Sento
The Japanese Public Bath
In Twilight Years

First Edition

Elizabeth Ann Ishiyama

ISBN: 978-0-615-26365-6

To Shingo
Your relentless drive and competitive spirit never fail to inspire me.

Contents

The Discovery 1
A Brief History 5
The Bath 11
The Subway Train 13
Asakusa 17
My Neighborhood Sanctuary 27
California Cool 37
Bathhouse Architecture 43
Rapid Changes 47
Ginza 53
Super Sento 59
The Traditional Sento 87
Tattoos and the Bath 91
The Boiler Man from Ikebukuro 97
Three Short Stories 103
A Force of Change 111

Reference Notes 115
Books 115
Sento 118
Printed Publications 121
Other Sources 121
Published Articles on the Internet 123
Internet Sites 124

A Message to the Reader

With this book, an attempt was made to capture a centuries-old Japanese tradition in its twilight years. In my research and visits to the public bath (*sento*) in Japan, I discovered that once again, the country is reinventing itself, transforming social behaviors and joining the worldwide club of cookie-cutter businesses in what's being touted as a global society. Add to that the erratic fluctuations in oil prices - along with Japan's low birthrate and you have a combination of forces that has put the neighborhood public bath on the fast track to extinction. My hope is that by sharing my thoughts and experiences, sento might be rediscovered, leading to a new appreciation and support for the humble business not only from the younger generation in Japan, but from the entire visiting world. For more information go to www.japansento.com.

Chapter 1

The Discovery

OK - I admit, I'm a bath taker. I've always cherished the bath, not only on cold days, but also as a part of my daily routine. I love to soak in hot water and watch the hypnotic swirl of nothingness move around me. Soaking to my shoulders in a mere tub of hot water refreshes my mind and recharges my body – and, simply put, it makes me feel good.

So why does a bath leave me feeling so refreshed and rejuvenated? Maybe it's the way the muscles relax in near zero gravity, or perhaps it has something to do with the thousands of negative ions and free electrons that manifest a vitalization function. As a woman of Northern European descent, I loosely attributed my routine to an ancestral link obscurely tied to my Viking and Celtic heritage, possibly having to do with some inherited genetic code. History documents that throughout the centuries, Northern Europeans regularly used natural hot springs and makeshift steam rooms to relax the mind and warm the body during the months of frigid temperatures. Originally, the steam rooms of the North were created by pouring cool water over heated rocks; more recently electric versions are installed inside the home. This mind and body treatment provides the same remedies many ancient cultures have subscribed to including the Romans, Turks, Native Americans and Japanese – to name a few.

For years, my version of the bath had been very American by filling a white porcelain tub with approximately forty gallons of hot tap water, lying reclined with my knees in the air and resting my neck and shoulders against a hard, cold surface. With this regular routine, I considered myself an expert soaker. That was, however, before I moved to Japan. In the fall of 2003, I moved to Tokyo at the invitation of a Japanese friend, which at the time I welcomed as an experiment. I was warned, "The country will either suck you in or spit you out. Without any expectations, I took a *carpe diem* plunge and seized the moment. It didn't take long before I found myself "sucked in" and embarked on a journey of discovery that included a serious exploration of sento, the Japanese public bath.

Despite my limited knowledge, I had a curiosity for things non-western, and began this delightful affair with a 400-year-old tradition that is so uniquely Japanese. One does not have to look too far to understand why Japanese people love hot water. Since ancient times, they've been raised on a plethora of natural hot springs which has provided a rich history of bathing. Located on an archipelago, the islands sit on one of the more active portions of the notorious "Ring of Fire," where the Pacific Plate and Philippine Plate are sub-ducted under the Asian Plate, resulting in the birth of many volcanoes. These hot spots contribute to almost 2000 natural hot springs seeping with minerals.

In modern Japan, the bath is an enjoyable discipline that has been refined to commendable heights, making the entire population true *masters of the bath*. Many Japanese bathe twice daily - once in the morning, and then again in the evening to wash away fatigue and promote good health. Different from the Westerners, Japanese have also acquired a taste for many unique and inventive ways to soak. The most popular is at a *ryokan*, an overnight inn with a hot water soaking tub located either in one's room, or in a nearby building. Sometimes the ryokan has a tub located outdoors called a *rotenburo*, which is especially enjoyable in much of the country's mountainous and coastal regions. The term *onsen* is associated with a bathing place in which the water is supplied by a natural hot spring (as opposed to heated tap water) and therefore is usually valued for its medicinal qualities. Many onsen locations in Japan date back hundreds of years with interesting and colorful histories, but they can also be new and modern establishments, located in a hotel or at a day spa. The new day spa business is growing in popularity, not only in Japan, but throughout the entire world, offering a long list of therapies designed to pamper every inch of the body. On a simpler note, there are sento, local neighborhood public baths that are distinctively Japanese. For approximately $4 USD (at today's rate of exchange), a sento will provide a safe and clean place to bathe and soak in an over-sized tub filled with wonderfully hot water. This type of bathhouse is found in a fair number of neighborhoods located in most of the country's major cities.

Before arriving in Tokyo, I'd only seen a sento depicted in a beautiful Japanese block print known as *ukiyo-e,* a scene I did not understand. It tweaked my curiosity - and without my knowing, gave me my first peek into the world of the public bath, with an introduction to hot water culture. The illustration showed women in kimono and one small child washing and socializing in a large room. A wooden bucket is filled with water along with smaller pails lying on the floor. Ukiyo-e roughly translates to "floating time" because the artist captures the world much like the lens of a camera, where the action of the day is frozen in detail using a wet brush and ink. This bathhouse print was exactly that: a day in the life at sento 200 years ago in *Edo*, now modern day Tokyo. As an interpretation of life on paper, ukiyo-e has provided historians and culture enthusiasts a great deal of insight into the past - not only to the customs and preferences of the day, but also to the etiquette and manners surrounding a society which at the time was virtually closed to the outside world.

Because I found this print scene so intriguing when I arrived in Japan, going to a public bath was on the top of my list of things to do. If I were going to understand this new and unfamiliar land and call it home, then a serious exploration of sento would be a good way to dive deeply into the foreign populace. Since the start of the feudal Edo-period in 1603 and continuing until the 1960's, going to sento was how most of the population in Japan bathed. At one time, the sento industry was comprised of nearly 10,000 privately owned, small businesses, but sadly it has seriously declined. With the implementation of modern plumbing, changes in social views and the unpredictable cost of oil, sento owners struggle to keep their doors open. Today's remaining sento are unique and quirky cultural jewels and no less a treasure in their twilight years. Over the course of a 5-year exploration, I became deeply passionate about their history, the architecture and the social benefits they still provide in

Japan's urban neighborhoods. After visiting nearly 70 different public baths, I'm saddened by the reality that the choice to soak at sento is *rapidly* diminishing. While the relatively few remaining bathhouses continue to function as a type of social glue, the complete disappearance looks inevitable. It's my opinion that such a loss will have a significant impact on Japanese society, with implications that affect the well-being of all future generations to come.

With the completion of this book in 2009, fewer than 900 sento (in Tokyo) were still open; and despite the unforgiving pressures to close, the remaining handful proudly maintained an irreplaceable tradition in a world that is becoming more homogenized and global. With all the benefits of shared culture, I don't think it's too narrow-minded to wish that some traditions never change. As a result of my visits, personal interviews and more than 2000 photographs, I wish I could put sento into a locked box and take possession of the key, ensuring all future generations could enjoy this public space – in the name of tradition.

I know that's not possible.

Chapter 2

A Brief History

For Japanese, the bath not only helps maintain their high standards of cleanliness, it also boosts their health and cleanses their souls. To better understand this, we should look at the history of bathing in Japan.

The first written description is Chinese and dates back to *The History of the Kingdom of Wei* (220 -265 A.D.). In brief, it makes reference to ritual bathing in Japan. Of all the Chinese records, the description appearing in this document is the most thorough, accounting for the beliefs and order of the day. Another later reference to bathing, compiled for the Japanese central government, can be found in the *Izumo Fudoki*, a book describing the natural features, culture and history of the region of Izumo, now Shimane Prefecture. It describes people using a hot spring for bathing and healing as early as 737 A.D.

The bath is also found at Buddhist temple compounds where designated buildings are built for washing and the purification of priests and Buddha statues. In ancient times, on occasion, these rooms were opened to the public, providing the opportunity for bathing known as *seyoku*, the provision of free baths that was often funded by wealthy patrons. In 1192 during the Kamakura-period, a powerful war lord offered a "charity bath" as a memorial service, which was recorded to have bathed 10,000 people over 100 days. Following this, and possibly due to the prior successful turn out, Todaiji Temple opened its bathhouse to the public in 1239. At Todaiji, a large iron tub two-meters in diameter, which was formally sunk in the ground, still remains as testimony to this public service. On the floor at the rear of the building, another large space is still visible where a cauldron is believed to have been placed to heat and supply hot water to the tub. The *seyoku* was invaluable to the hygiene of all sectors of society, not to mention as a source of enjoyment.

In addition, water is used ritualistically in both major Japanese religions. In the Shinto religion, a highly structured, spiritual practice indigenous to Japan, cleansing the mouth and hands with water is performed before prayer, while in more celebrated events, using a river, the sea or a waterfall is a type of bathing is known as *misogi* which removes impurities from the body, mind and spirit. The *yamabushi* Buddhist monks who reside secluded in the mountains, famously practice their discipline of sitting under the falling water, chilled from melted snow, deep in chant and meditation.

The earliest confirmed, written record of the word *sento* being used to describe a public bath can be traced to 1266, listed in the Nichieren Buddhist document as a "small money bath." This document, however, doesn't say exactly when public bathhouses started operating as independent businesses (not associated with a temple), although in more recent history we can trace them to Edo. From here sento evolved and endured over the following centuries as a public service used by a wide range of classes as an established daily washing routine.

According to the Tokyo Bath Association, a public bath building was built near *Edobashi* (Edo Bridge) in 1591, and is thought to have been the first "pay-for-bath" service in the city. Edo had yet to become the official seat of government, so the town had little importance until Tokugawa Ieyasu, the first of the Tokugawa Shoguns (the guardian General of the Emperor) made it a capital in 1603. With the start of a new and powerful Tokugawa era, tidal marshes were filled in, an increase of population drove a healthy commerce and the castle was enlarged to become the biggest in the land.

By the mid 18th century, Edo had become the country's major center for domestic trade, arts and political authority, with a pay-for-bath sento in every neighborhood. The city's population was approximately 1.5 million people, and its residents were living without indoor plumbing. In fact, the Shogun discouraged the use of baths in private homes because of the unsafe methods used to heat

6

water. When fire broke out, which happened on many occasions, the wooden city quickly became a dangerous and uncontrollable inferno, something everyone feared.

The early bathhouse was called *yuya* and was more of a steam bath. One had to enter by crouching low under a double sliding door at the entrance, known as a *zakuroguchi,* a cleft doorway low in height to keep the steam from escaping. The rooms were also very dark, so dark bathers actually cleared their throats to signal their presence to avoid bumping into other bathers. Customers would sit with legs dangling in the hot water while their upper bodies became damp with the rising hot steam. The tub was nearly at ground level with a small kindled fire that burned under a protective plate. This closet style steam bath, or *todanaburo* as it was called, was a place of mixed bathing - used by men and women, young and old alike. The people of Edo were more open-minded about public nudity compared to today's populace, but it's also important to understand that nudity helped equalize a population that was highly structured and extremely class conscious. Today, bathing nude in the presence of others, *hadaka no tsukiai* (naked friendship), is considered a respectful way to show you have nothing to hide and are willing to reveal the naked truth about yourself. Everyday in Japan the country's top corporate executives practice hadaka no tsukiai at notoriously expensive golf clubs by jumping into a large tub of hot water together after 18 holes on the course and talking about their shots and scores.

Towards the later part of the Edo era, the two-story bathhouse with hot water on the ground floor and large rooms for relaxing built above proliferated. On the top floor, patrons enjoyed stretching out on *tatami,* a woven straw mat flooring, to sip sake (or tea), socialize and enjoy a chess like board game of *shoogi* or *go.* At some locations, "service women" were employed by the sento owners to wash the backs of male patrons. For a brief time, this led to evening female prostitutes moving in which created a short list of sento that functioned as a sort of gentleman's *club,* despite the dismay from the Shogun. Prostitution was supposed to stay inside the walls of Yoshiwara, an entertainment district near the downtown neighborhood of Asakusa. But history tells us that wasn't always the case. Even with the Shogun attempting to ban the activity, not until the devastating earthquake of 1703, for some undocumented reason, when the businesses were rebuilt, did the ladies of ill repute disappear.

At the close of the 18th century, about 600 sento provided a place for city dwellers of various classes to bathe, relax and communicate with neighbors. The simple beginnings of sento had become the firm foundation of a daily routine and valuable hygiene, as well as the nerve center of communication and local gossip! In the mid to late 1800's, sweeping cultural changes began to take place in Japan, resulting from internal shifts of power away from Shogunate rule as well as industrial modernism and Western puritanical overtones. These major changes define the Meiji-period, a time of rapid modernization, sometimes referred to as the period of Europeanization which lasted from 1868 to 1905. At this point in history, the newly established government did away with many practices from feudal times, including mixed bathing at sento in an effort to make Japan appear "more Western" in the eyes of its new global neighbors. To help meet this new expectation, a center wall inside the wash area was incorporated to divide the sexes and double as advertisement space sold to local businesses. Early on, these dividing walls had a small hole to provide means of passing soap back and forth between family members. Bathtubs became larger; and to keep the water clean, the tub had been raised so that the bather had to "step up" into the bath. By the end of Meiji-period, the zakuroguchi had been removed and the steam was directed out a pipe, exiting through the roof. A new bath was developed called a *teppoburo* (rifle bath) in which the fire source was moved to a separate room and iron pipes safely transported the hot water to large centralized tubs. The continuation of steady improvements made business grow so that by the end of the 19th century, the public bath had become quite an established industry. Soon an Association was formed which provided guidance along with the enforcement of regulatory standards regarding bathhouse equipment and hygiene.

The Taisho-period, or democracy era which followed Meiji, continued to bring even more changes to sento. Tile replaced the wood floors (further improving hygiene) and by the 1920's and 30's, the installation of individual hot and cold faucets created personal wash stations that became commonplace. The additional improvement of sophisticated boilers also enabled businesses to more efficiently pump hot water into even larger and more spacious soaking tubs, providing fresh water daily. According to the Sento Association, bathhouses reached their peak in 1968, with approximately 2,687 establishments operating in Tokyo; and 10,000, nationwide. However, by 2008, that number had dwindled to roughly 3,000 countrywide, and less than 900 operating in "old Edo." Due to yet another new era of cultural changes and for other reasons examined in this book, nationwide, nearly 300 sento establishments go out of business every year. Obviously, if this trend continues, a centuries-old tradition will soon be gone forever.

Elizabeth Ann Ishiyama

Chapter 3

The Bath

Within days of landing in Japan, I quickly realized that "the bath" was not only different from anything I'd used before, but soaking in hot water was part of the national lifestyle. In this water rich country, it's essentially a daily routine for Japanese to indulge in a primal form of regal pampering. In the home, the wash area and the bathtub are in an encapsulated room, a self-contained design that allows for the bath water to be filled to the top of the tub and spill over to the floor without worry. When getting into a freshly poured tub, one hears a forceful sound of falling water gushing over the edge, briefly levitating just about anything left on the floor. The overflow, which is cleverly directed to a drain, enhances the aroma of the bath water that's been sprinkled with agents made from pine needle or various flowers. These bath powders are so widely used they are sold at virtually all convenience stores, pharmacies, super markets and dollar stores. Even individual, hot-spring locations market their own fancy, private label brands sold at a hefty price. Soon after sitting, silence takes over as the water line hovers just above the shoulders, completing a simple act of decadence that reminds me of pouring Dom Perignon Champagne into a crystal flute and letting the sparkling wine spill over the rim.

Japan's bathtub and toilet (also equipped with a water bidet) are generally not housed in the same room, providing another example of a society seemingly obsessed with cleanliness. Plainly speaking, this makes a lot of sense and might call for a re-examination of the bathroom floor plan common to the West. Inside the walls of Japan's tiny living spaces, there's no skimping on space for the wash and tub area. And why not? This essential space, in many ways, defines a standard of living.

The bathtub in Japan is also deeper by design, and many are equipped with temperature-control dials and electronic filters. The water is used multiple times. Strange as that may sound, the water is kept clean by a washing routine performed before entering the bath. Call it "earth friendly," "island mentality," or just good practice in "water conservation" - this measure saves hundreds of millions of gallons of water every year. There can be little argument that other progressive nations should have a look at ways of adopting similar efficiencies of water use.

Chapter 4

The Subway Train

Within days of my arrival to Tokyo, I wasted no time in seeking my first public bath experience. The arrangement to visit a sento was made possible through an introduction. I was to be carefully managed by a gracious woman named Reiko Oyama. She was a young mother of two, willing to accompany me on an introductory outing and provide a lesson in proper, public bathhouse etiquette. Under her careful watch, I learned the rules and customs that, for a Westerner, are quite unfamiliar. The plan was to go to a sento located in her Asakusa neighborhood, the *old downtown* of Edo.

Before Tokyo was the capital, it was comprised of small fishing villages with a river that fed into the large surrounding bay. In the 18th year of Tensho (1590), Tokugawa Ieyasu was appointed Shogun by the Emperor after defeating the Hideyori loyalists in the battle of Sekigahara. With a mission to end civil fighting, he established a powerful seat in Edo and designated Asakusa as a portion of his claim with boundaries equal to 90,000 liters of rice. With the start of Tokugawa rule, a line of Shoguns succeeded and maintained absolute control of entire Japan. Interestingly, during this period many disciplines were refined and reinvented to fit the highly structured feudal rule, which resulted in a standard of excellence and adherences to quality still maintained today. Refinement unfolded in areas of martial arts, swordsmanship, dance, leisure, food, music and theater - a cultivation of a "new self" that came directly from the communities expanding from the downtown borough of Asakusa. Today, Edo-period culture is still strong in this part of the city, prevalent in the traditional vocations, food and year-round festivals that attract large crowds from both home and overseas. The residents of Asakusa are especially proud of their past and consider themselves as *Edo-kko,* the children of Edo.

For my excursion, I received quick verbal instructions regarding the train line and approximate travel time. It was to be my first "solo" adventure across the city using Japan's illustrious rail system. I would leave at 11:15am and should expect to arrive in Asakusa just before noon. Reiko-san would be waiting under the shadow of the Asahi Beer building, identifiable by the enormous, golden flame sculpture on the roof. Originally, the sculpture artist had intended the flame to sit side-by-side with two other golden adornments. He envisioned the sculpted shapes would resemble the action of a flame, high above the contemporary black glass building. Unfortunately for safety concerns, two of the flames were removed, leaving something that resembles an over-sized piece of *poop,* forty-eight stories above the traditional neighborhood. This "golden turd," as it's affectionately called, can be seen from many vantage points, thus making it a popular and easy-to-find landmark that many in the city use.

The Asakusa line departing from the Mita station would give me a straight shot, meaning no platform changes required. When I arrived at the station, I referred to the large, color-coded route map mounted on the wall near the gate. For the new user, the number of subway lines can be very confusing. I watched seasoned rail riders jumping off to the side, quickly checking the map, and then jumping back into the flow without missing a beat. As I stood staring at the weave of color, I could feel the blood rushing to my head as I thought, "Oh my gosh! Which red line was it again?" People were passing in both directions as if I'd hit the *fast-forward button* on life. The pressure from all the physical rush of hurried passengers darting and cutting in front of me was like being in the middle of a returning school of pacific coast salmon with a single minded focus: move forward. In the confusion, I took my chances on a best guess and away I went.

On the train was a sea of Tokyo's mid-week office workers dressed in navy blue, charcoal gray and black. Mostly in the company of men, I sat as they fiddled with their phones, read soft-covered, pocket-sized books and slept with their foreheads in a full tilt. The number of slumbering individuals far exceeded those awake as the cluster of connected cars hummed across the underground tracks. Japanese commuters have this amazing skill of sitting shoulder-to-shoulder in crowded trains, napping like cats and miraculously waking just before their stop is announced. Moving from station to station below street level for 40 minutes, the train finally emerged back into daylight and I realized something was very wrong. We had crossed over a river, and the view out the window looked more and more like a suburb with plots of well-tended farmland, separated by clusters of small housing developments. I was sure I'd missed my stop. I had half expected to get lost, because most of the time I can't find my way out of a box! At the next stop, I exited on to an outdoor platform and felt slightly panicked. Using my cell phone, I called the person who had arranged the introduction and gave him a heads up to my mistake. I asked if he could help me reschedule the outing with Reiko-san for another day.

"I'm having some trouble finding my way," I explained, "It's probably best to reschedule."

"Reschedule? That's impossible," he replied. "You must find a way to succeed – Reiko-san is waiting for you!"

This apparent no-empathy position coupled with a "you-can't-quit" attitude felt very unfair. Maybe the harsh tone was an example of the steadfastness famous in Japanese culture. Before I could ask again to wiggle out of my commitment, he went on to say,

"If you say you're going to do something, then you have to do it. You must fulfill your words."

This wasn't what I expected! No silly excuses were going to be accepted here. So, hanging on tight to my emotions, I had no other choice but to take a corrective action and try again. I felt I was getting a strong dose of the highly-regarded Japanese samurai *bushido* code that stressed honor, self-discipline, and bravery. At that moment I felt anything but brave. I *do* have a sense of honor and I *do* have strong self-discipline. After all, I descended from Viking and Celtic stock, infamous for organized attacks by water under the cover of darkness. But my ancestors' history was far from this strange eastern land, and at that moment, all I wished for was something more familiar. I put on a brave face, picked up my imaginary sword and got back on the train heading in the opposite direction. Finally, I arrived under the golden flame at 2pm which, in hindsight, gave me a valuable lesson: Survival in this city meant the train needed to become my best friend, hopefully, sooner than later.

Chapter 5

Asakusa

Reiko-san was with her 6-year-old son Yuzo, and 4-year-old daughter Shoko, who were still smiling after waiting so patiently. I'm sure they wondered if I was made of the right stuff to call Tokyo my home. With my confidence shaken, I questioned that too! Reiko-san took over the navigation and drove us back to her apartment where we'd pick up a few supplies for our sento visit. Feeling quite embarrassed, I apologized for my extreme tardiness. We zipped through the downtown traffic and I realized my first solo experience was, to say the least, disastrous. I was strangely thankful I'd been pushed out of my comfort zone and not given up, although I wasn't ready to say that out loud. I just needed a little more practice.

As Reiko-san parked the car, I thought about the phrase, "women drivers," often heard from the mouths of men in the States. It wouldn't hold any water here! Reiko-san was brilliant with the maneuvers required to back up between two cars without a centimeter to spare. I was definitely in the hands of a real "child of Edo," which during my weak moment, made me feel strong. We quickly grabbed soap, towels and shampoo and continued to sento on foot.

In many parts of Tokyo, the city can appear commercial, loud and brash. Especially in the major districts where super-sized screens project a bombardment of messages and advertisements in between rows of neon that reach double digit heights. In addition, lively sidewalk banter comes from merchants and employees calling out their business specials. Their amazing vocal talent is a high-spirited sales pitch with a unique style. It might go something like; *"Welcome! Welcome! Please enjoy our delicious taste! Welcome! Welcome!"* The words flow in a catchy jingle, projecting excitement and enthusiasm, tempting the passer-by to stop and make a purchase. This constant drum of "Hey listen to this, Hey try this. Hey buy this," coupled with the multitude of blinking, flashing lights is at best taxing unless kept to small doses.

In contrast, Asakusa was more low-key with shorter buildings and narrow streets filled with friendly merchants nodding hello as we walked by. The storefronts were free of hawkers and situated among a large assortment of potted plants that dotted the sidewalks with a rainbow of color. Edo culture evolved directly from these very streets. I could feel a deep connection to the past, knowing the residents proudly keep that golden era alive, not only in their hearts and minds, but also in the nearby sumo training stables, the traditional arts, and the many festivals that thrive in this neighborhood. The primary method for attracting customers was with the quiet swing of the cotton *noren* hanging just above the business doorways. When hanging, this split-curtain fabric works in partnership with the wind, moving the panels back and forth like a silent message board. People who pass by easily see that the establishment is open for business.

As we made our way, Reiko-san seemed to know many of the people; and a polite exchange of greetings took place which even Shoko-chan, the youngest child performed with grown-up respect. When we arrived at the entrance of the sento, the noren was hanging on a bamboo pole printed with the kanji character pronounced "yu," indicating hot water. The mandatory shoe removal area was just a step off the sidewalk, forming the front entry to the business. This designated shoe space, known as a *genkan,* is found at the entrance of many Japanese dwellings. It's the place where one removes shoes before proceeding into the living area. The custom of removing footwear in Japan goes back to the Heian-period (794 – 1192) when it was a common practice among the upper classes. Gradually it spread to all of society. The main reason that footwear is shed in this fashion is of course because it's the most practical way to keep a living space clean, especially during *tsuyu,* Japan's rainy season. Also the Japanese custom of sitting and sleeping directly on the tatami floor gives further practicality to the established manner. Shoe removal takes place not only in the home, but also in certain types of restaurants, offices and schools.

All three family members had taken on the roll of "tour guide" and were eager to show me just how to stow my shoes in a wall locker called the *getabako*. This word directly translates to "sandal box" and is commonly found in many public spaces. Here, they lined both sides of the entry, each with a square wallet-sized wooden key in the locking devices. From the floor to nearly 6-feet high, the storage provided an entryway free of clutter. These organized spaces keep in line with Japan's minimalist design tendencies.

Watching my guides quickly remove their shoes gave me yet another reminder that footwear in Japan must come off as easily as it goes on. This is why I'd seen so many "slip on" styles! Both Yuzo-kun and Shoko-chan giggled as I struggled with the box. My attempt to close the door had me pushing and opening and pushing and opening, because it wouldn't shut with my big, American shoe size 10!

Visiting Westerners notice almost immediately the actual size of things in Japan is much smaller. To my eyes, all these tiny things look so cute, or *kawaii*, a Japanese word heard endless times a day - especially in the phrase, *"kawaii desu ne"* meaning "It's cute - isn't it!" The differences one might expect to see are in the size of vehicles and apartments; but everyday items such as shopping carts, drink containers, food packaging and even toothbrushes are all well...so *Kawaii!* Even the toy dog breeds seen so often sitting in handbags or doggy strollers, wearing tiny hats and tiny coats fashioned after designer labels, are so "kawaii desu ne!"

With a slight upward tilt of my shoes, and one more extra firm push on the door, the getabako finally closed. I removed the flat key and followed Reiko-san and the kids through the door marked *onna* for women. This would be the first kanji character I'd commit to memory so as not to later embarrass myself when I visited sento alone.

A clerk (in this case a woman) known as the *bandai,* politely greeted us and collected my 400 yen (approximately $3.80 USD). She sat in an elevated chair and performed the function of cashier with all the arriving customers. Her 3-foot across space doubled as a place from which to keep the business in order with a birds-eye view of both the men's and women's locker areas. With a full unobstructed view of people dressing and undressing, the bandai does emit some sort of weird power that could possibly be unsettling for the modest individual. More so if the bandai is of the opposite sex.

The interior of the Asakusa sento was strangely frozen in time. The combination of the dark faux-wood paneling and a large coin-operated, hair-drying chair, adorned with its bullet shaped dome screamed 1965! I'd not seen one of these hair dryers since I was a little girl, back when I used to visit my Grandma Ruby's beauty shop in Des Moines, Iowa. I can remember the "pin curl perms" she prepared for the neighborhood ladies, followed by sitting them under the same enormous domes. It was nearly impossible for the women to have a conversation because the darn things were so loud! While they flipped the pages of magazines, making animated hand gestures, their occasional outburst of laughter wearing a head full of plastic pink and green rollers left quite an impression on me. After what seemed like hours of drying time, my Grandma would eventually turn off the blower and complete the final steps of their beauty treatment using a round brush, a black comb and *lots* of hairspray. When the last customer left, my younger brother, Billy, and I would play "hair stylist." I would insist Billy sit under the large metal dome while I made believe he was my customer. Sometimes I went as far as giving him a few snips with the pin-point scissors that were always left lying around. Seeing the monstrous dryer brought to life memories I'd stored in the archives of my mind and played back like an old familiar movie not seen in years.

The sento floor was a chocolate brown, shiny and smooth from years of wear. The mono-chromatic color scheme continued to the paneled walls, with larger wooden lockers sitting side-by-side like rabbit hutches. These were providing a place to stash street clothes while one soaked in the bath. I sat on a narrow wooden bench and began to disrobe, eyeing a stack of tattered, well-read magazines, a selection of flat paper fans and a "very used" drink cooler. I would later come to know that these three things are always found inside sento. The electric cooler box was something one would expect to find at a gas station on the old Route 66 in eastern Arizona; but unlike the Cokes and Sprites, this had a variety of unfamiliar drinks in glass, aluminum and wax cardboard containers. The green and brown teas were identifiable, but the tiny plastic bottles filled with a milky liquid, which could be consumed in two gulps, looked very peculiar. These bottles were faced five wide and five deep, like an army of 3-inch high soldiers in opaque orange uniforms standing at attention. Their peel-off foil tops reminded me of a time when milk was delivered in glass bottles and left at the doorsteps of homes. One would hope the crows didn't find the bottles before bringing them in.

There was an ancient-looking green, metal floor scale standing next to a sliding glass door. Women were stepping on to the jiggling platform and the needle settled on their weight while the bandai took little notice, as if she were invisible. Just across the room, a glass and chrome display case under the bright fluorescent lights sported bars of soap, combs, towels and shavers. All were neatly displayed in classic, vintage packaging. Probably, many were long-time trusted brands that have been a part of the sento world for years. I would think most sales were made from the customer who forgot to pack an essential item.

The four of us removed all our clothing and were ready to go into the tub area located just beyond the steamy sliding glass door. I imagined that going to sento would be the very first memory children in Japan have of communal, nude bathing, a custom that no doubt helps contribute to a society accepting itself personally and interpersonally. It was interesting to compare the differences between the East and the West, considering complete nudity in a public space is almost nonexistent in the West. Westerners do not spend much time socializing in the nude. In our western changing areas, one often has the option of dressing and undressing *behind curtain pulls*. We are far more prudish than the Japanese, mostly due to the influence of the Catholic Church, which at one time in history considered the display of the body as evil and to be avoided at all costs. During the early Middle Ages, a time when society was strongly patriarchal and dominated by priests, repressive attitudes toward nakedness sparked an organized "fig-leaf campaign" that

21

went so far as to cover nudity in fine art. These extreme periods still carry over to our more modern times, as the Church continues to play a major role in defining our western behavior. Japan seemed refreshingly free from this influence, providing a naked truth to one's own existence. Currently however, there are discussions among Japanese who believe as more and more younger people bathe *only at home*, they will not be properly socialized without the "skinship" or experience of mutual nakedness.

In the wash area, I could see four women sitting side-by-side along the tiled wall which was equipped with individual hot and cold water spouts. Above each pair of faucets was a mirror and shower head, approximately a meter from the floor. With an unrealistic wish to blend in, I mirrored Reiko-san's move by grabbing one of the small plastic stools along with a round bowl from a stack next to the door. The stool was no larger than 10-inches high with a 3-inch hole at the top, making it easy to lift from the knee-high tower and carry across the room. But was I really expected to sit on this? Looking around, I saw one woman sitting on a stool, while three others knelt on the tile floor, sitting on the backs of their heels. Should I sit on the floor, or sit on a stool? I stand nearly 5-feet 8-inches tall, with *not-so-perfect* knees; so sitting anywhere near the ground is a challenging position for me. Once I sat down, would I be able to stand back up? And furthermore, it wasn't just a matter of getting up or down. The actual sitting area on top of the stool seemed terribly short on room. Feeling a bit like I had entered the surreal world of Alice in Wonderland, I made the decision to sit on the stool and risk a probable embarrassing moment. Leaning over at the waist, I placed the palms of my hands on the edge, centered my body and squatted down in a very unrefined motion. **Kur-plunk**! Thankful I'd landed on the stool and not the floor, I looked around with somewhat of a show-off grin, feeling for a brief moment as if I looked like someone who'd done this before. Reiko-san proceeded to demonstrate how to fill the round bowl with water, pushing the knobs towards the wall, alternating between hot and cold. I filled my bowl with the perfect temperature and began a complete head-to-toe pre-wash, required before entering the hot water. Without doubt, this was the most important of all public bath manners, followed by NO SOAP IN THE TUB. Just when I thought I was clean, Reiko-san and the kids were soaping up for a second time, using a sliding technique, back to soap then forward to rinse, slide, soap, slide, rinse – and repeat. That was the drill.

The soaking room measured approximately 35-feet wide by 25-feet deep, with enough individual washing stations to accommodate 16 people. There was a very high wooden ceiling that reached its peak in the center, sloping back down over to the men's side. A half wall down the middle of the room divided the men from the women. It ran from the bandai booth back to the far wall where the tubs were located. The height of this partition was just a few feet above a person who might stand 6-feet tall, so the open-air top allowed for sound to travel back and forth. I could hear the low chatter of men on the other side, which no doubt for centuries has provided a great source of neighborhood gossip! Reiko-san motioned me to get up from my ground perch and join her and the kids in one of the soaking tubs. I acknowledged her with a nod and waited until she looked away, in an effort to disguise my rise...just in case! Examining the shower head in front of me, I wondered what would happen if I grabbed it for leverage. But first I'd try to reverse my motion. With fierce concentration and pushing up with the palms of my hands, *voila* - I was up! Masking my surprise, I walked to the back wall where the kids were testing the water with their hands.

Both tubs were lined with tiles, each large enough to comfortably seat 6 adults. The tub on the left was filled with water that bubbled vigorously, while the attached tub to the right was quiet and had a floating sack of herbs that turned the water a dark red. I was told the herbal remedy would help prevent some sort of intestinal trouble. (Hum....how does that work?). I decided first to try the jet tub and glanced at the round wall-mounted thermometer positioned a few inches above the water line. It was pegged at 43-degrees Celsius. "Uh-oh...Celsius" - a vague memory surfaced from a 1970's push by the California school system to move away from using Fahrenheit and adopt a form of measurement that *only the rest of the world was using!* This was the same failed attempt to replace feet and inches with the metric system. Both plans were abandoned as quickly as they were started. So, needless to say, I couldn't calculate the exact conversion. My familiarity with Jacuzzi water in the United States had me assume it would be in a range of 98 to 102-degrees Fahrenheit.

Putting one leg in the tub, my inner voice yelled "Whoa – That's HOT!" Looking at two women who were already sitting neck high in the water, I thought, "How can this be?" With caution, I continued slowly adding my other leg. "No way!" I wanted to shout, contemplating a fast exit out of the *human stew pot*. In the middle of deciding what to do, another woman well into her 80's entered the tub in one fluid motion and sat with the water line touching her chin. So just how did she do that? Maybe, just maybe, she wanted to subtly demonstrate her Japanese strength. Well I'll be the first to say I was impressed. I found the inner strength to lower my body until I too had the water lapping at my chin. Our squinting eyes softly met, and in a delicate match of wits, we were soon transported to a dreamy and almost euphoric state, enjoying what millions have done for centuries before us - relaxing in very hot water. I knew from that moment on, soaking at sento was for me. After two complete rounds of in and out of the tub, my first official visit was complete, leaving me totally rejuvenated and remarkably refreshed.

As we were getting back into our street clothes, Yuzo-kun took a great interest in my cell phone which I'd left lying on the bench. With a slide and a twist, the phone transformed like an animated figure into a digital camera. Because it was new, I had yet to figure out all the seemingly complicated features and functions, so I worried little about a 6-year-old picking it up. However, it was only a matter of seconds before he was in full camera mode and taking pictures inside the dressing area! Oh my gosh, this was serious. Just beyond my locker I could see a poster hanging on the wall with a drawing of a cell phone inside the universal red circle and slash. It was clearly making the point that the use of cell phones was not permitted, not to mention taking pictures inside the sento. Knowing this had crossed the line, I didn't want to be blamed for any possible trouble, but at the same time, felt uncomfortable and out of place taking action to stop his behavior. Just then, a nearly naked woman next to us bent over and spoke to Yuzo-kun in a soft voice, steadily giving him an ear full of instruction. He carefully listened to in a stiff and attentive manner. It seemed clear he was being told politely yet directly, that he needed to stop this picture taking *immediately*. Not for one moment did Reiko-san look concerned or show signs of distress. Her confidence beamed as she allowed the woman to make her points, looking quite comfortable with the entire situation. Yuzo-kun put the camera down, showed me a mischievous smile and went back to the business of getting dressed.

Even in one of the world's largest cities, the sento was a small town community center where neighbors were not afraid to get involved and take part in shaping future generations. From this incident I could see the importance and benefits of providing a forum for elders to leave their stamp on society. The public bathhouse provided Reiko-san and her family with a deep sense of community, an essential component of any well-balanced life. This was far better than a wave from the car or the occasional encounter at the market, or even a chance meeting at the local coffee house. The sento was different. It was a unique place where wisdom, earned only by years, could interact directly with the younger generation, thereby tightening the threads that make up the fabric of a complex and able society.

Elizabeth Ann Ishiyama

Chapter 6

My Neighborhood Sanctuary

Settling into a Japanese lifestyle in the heart of Tokyo is by far one of the most interesting transitions an American can make. Having previously lived in a medley of suburbs that included San Francisco, Seattle, Portland (Oregon), and Los Angeles, I'd yet to experience *real city living*. I'd always dreamed about living in Manhattan, and now I found everything I imagined the Big Apple would offer was at my doorstep in Tokyo. This Asian metropolis is constantly in motion and more and more people are moving here every year. In the very near future, demographically it's projected to be the largest city in the world. All this living, working and playing creates a blur of activity; yet despite the millions of inhabitants, it's incredibly civilized and safe, with a cleanliness standard that deserves a study all by itself. Tokyo is a living example of a culture that has adapted to explosive growth with an outwardly cooperative attitude. Without any doubt, I was earning a degree in city living and felt fortunate to gain my official status in this part of the world. Instead of taking a bite out of the Big Apple, I was enjoying a slice of a tasty Japanese *mikan* – a fruit more commonly known in the West as the mandarin orange, arguably the most popular fruit in Japan; and just like the city itself, is a treat enjoyed in so many ways.

A break from the fervor is always welcomed even with an intense love for city life. I'd learned the public bathhouse was the perfect escape. It's nearly unmatched by any other public space, providing a walled sanctuary that wasn't only tranquil but was also an authentic force of balance in a busy world. With my newly-acquired public bath manners, I was ready to venture out alone and find more sento to experience; however, after my recent episode to Asakusa, I thought it best (for the time being) to stay off the tracks. The closest sento in my neighborhood was only a 15-minute walk from my apartment, located in the shadow of Keio University, the country's oldest private University founded in 1858. It was there I found *Manzai-yu*, a humble public bathhouse nestled off the main walking street.

This neighborhood is small, but it bustles with walkers, bicycles and scooters. Merchants are selling from tiny storefronts and there's a good share of counter-style eateries and noisy pachinko parlors. Playing pachinko is somewhat of a national obsession in Japan. Adults gamble with their money on a belief they can beat the odds of an electronic machine. Once played on a simple pin-ball like mechanism, today's players pour hard earned *yen* into what closely resembles a Vegas slot machine.

This macro economy comfortably shares its space with a large assortment of transportation services, some domestic retail chains and the mega company NEC, whose "Super Tower" casts a shadow on the two and three-story surrounding neighborhood structures. Because this area of Tokyo is diverse in class, I imagined the customers at Manzai-yu would be as well. Most likely a mix of long-time residents, students and port workers – all who call this part of Tokyo home. I arrived in front of the sento at 3pm, only to discover it didn't open for another hour. No problem. Exploring the neighborhood would be fun. This is one of the countless neighborhoods found tucked away and out of sight, adjacent to the city's major arteries – the core essence of what makes this city so great.

I headed to the winding backstreet designed for pedestrians only. At that time of day, many of the restaurants removed the noren curtain indicating they were closed, while inside the owners and employees ate a late lunch and made preparations for the evening crowd. Passing a game center, it was full of male students who were attending the nearby, 2-year technical school, a sound alternative for many young adults who don't enroll in traditional University. Smartly dressed in their dark suits and ties, these 20-somethings were wildly engaged in the center's assortment of electronic entertainment. The mandatory dress code (especially with the tie) made them appear so professional. For many boys and girls in Japan, the school uniform is still compulsory, leaving self-expression to be demonstrated in other ways, like changing hair color for example. With all shades of brown to blond, the cuts are creative and often laborious to maintain. A stop inside any train station bathroom will give one an idea of the time and effort put into this daily hair presentation. Even boys in Tokyo carefully manage their hair with a fair amount of gel and hairspray, appearing quite fashionable but also more feminine than young men in the West. Many even go so far as to pluck and shape their eyebrows into carefully crafted arches, which can also be dyed to match to color of their hair color. Much of the style influence comes from the popular *boy bands* in Japan which not only help define fashion, but widely shape the sound of today's J-pop music scene. This "packaged look and sound" resonates throughout the country, and, I might add, is strong in many other parts of Asia as well. Another possible contributing factor may just merely be a result of pushing too much conformity at an impressionable age, underscored by the requirement of a school uniform. However, dressing in the same apparel lessens the awareness of class and softens the potential negative implications in a society where this distinction carries a lot of weight. I think about how sento also strips away these clues, making it more difficult to determine one's social *rank* while inside the bathhouse – and I think that's good.

I kept walking with people of all ages hurrying about me, dashing in and out of a variety of stores, most of which specialized in one core product or service. From the store that sells business cards (held in high regard in Japan) to the custom tailored military-style school uniform, this "one item" focus creates real specialty shops, with notably high levels of service and product knowledge. Much of American shopping is at the "Big Box Retailers" like Target, Wal-Mart and Costco - incredibly convenient yes, but don't expect much when you ask a store clerk for help. Japan's neighborhood communities still make an attempt to support the small merchant, but one can see this is getting more difficult as the trend to build larger mass merchandisers and mega stores is making its way east. Earlier in the week an article in the Daily Yomiuri newspaper reported that Japan's largest supermarket operator, Seiyu Ltd., had recently opened a pilot "Super Center" in Shizuoka Prefecture; and without surprise, it noted that Wal-Mart held a controlling stake in the venture. It went on to read that more than 500 customers burst into the 8,000 square-meter sales floor the minute it opened. With its 30 cash registers, shoppers could now purchase an entire range of products and pay all at once - a relatively new concept for Japanese. From reading the newspaper review, the test store seemed to be off to a popular start which I would say represents another sign of change coming to Japan's macro economies. Lucky for me, "Big Box Mania" had not yet infiltrated this neighborhood because I could still find a local fishmonger, a noodle stand, a tofu vendor as well as plenty of well-stocked independently owned bookstores, catering to the country's insatiable hunger for the printed page.

As the time approached 4pm, I made my way back to Manzai-yu with a new twinge of apprehensiveness. I'd been told about some trouble at a bathhouse in northern Japan where they'd once made a policy to bar *non-Japanese looking people* from entering. After reading the television transcripts from a documentary produced by NHK (Nihon Hoso Kyokai), Japan's gigantic public broadcast network, I had a greater understanding of the reason why this happened in Otaru, the city near Sapporo on the island of Hokkaido. In Otaru, non-Japanese make up less than 1% of the population. The owner of the bathhouse claimed that visiting Russian sailors had displayed poor bath manners which threatened his business, thus sparking a JAPANESE ONLY policy. This exclusion policy then spread to a number of onsen in the area which at certain times of the year are awash with Russian sailors. Russian fisherman also arrive from Sakhalin and Primorye and dock nearby to unload their catch of crab and octopus. At its closest point, the Northern Japanese island of Hokkaido is separated from Russia by a mere 43-kilometers. Since the end of the Cold War, people of all walks of Russian life have been visiting this island for recreation and shopping.

Of the approximately 45 public bathing facilities in this area, one onsen in particular was put under the media microscope with a nationwide audience when it began to refuse entry to people who *looked* non-Japanese. The onsen complained that because visiting

Russian sailors had been drinking in the bathhouse, swimming in the tubs and using loud voices, the local Japanese customers did not want to mix with *gaijin* (outsiders) in the bath. The owner said he had begun receiving calls from his regulars to check if any non-Japanese were present before coming. I can imagine how the hot bath owner felt, but the makeshift policy was most definitely discriminatory and wrong. As I read the transcripts, it was clear that the differences in culture posed a challenge for the people of Otaru, and the "Japanese Only" policy was a side effect of a much more complex issue that had most likely simmered under the surface for years.

Arudou Debito, born in the United States, along with two of his foreign friends had become victims of this makeshift rule and took legal action to change the policy. Debito was not only raising a family in Hokkaido but had also formally taken a Japanese name and citizenship. All three foreigners forced the JAPANESE ONLY policy to a national level discussion with a claim against the onsen. The city's judicial system made the decision that "excluding people because they *look foreign* is not acceptable in the eyes of the Japanese judiciary" and ordered payment by the defendant of 1,000,000 yen (approximately $10,000 USD) to each plaintiff for damages. The attempted appeal was rejected by the Supreme Court of Japan, hopefully setting a new precedence for bathhouse and onsen owners throughout the country. The trouble in Otaru had publicly exposed the feelings some Japanese have about foreigners. Race and cultural differences are a major issue in all parts of the world, and Japan is no different. Why was I worried? This wasn't Otaru and I wasn't a Russian sailor. Still my mind was racing with self-induced fear, likely fueled by going to sento alone for the first time.

In front of Manzai-yu, I joined a queue of elderly Japanese men and women patiently waiting for the doors to open. Bingo! Real people were living out a centuries-old tradition right here in my Keio neighborhood. So, this really was a part of daily life for people in Japan – and I was going to be a part of it. Everyone looked well past their 60's and my presence undoubtedly was a bit curious. But we all had one thing in common: a desire to enjoy the art of soaking. This sento had a very simple appearance marked by a modest nylon banner with the badly faded hot water kanji character. The unpolished entry floor was well-worn, and the now familiar shoe lockers faced the street. Many people passed by, taking little notice of our line that stretched out along the building. Holding true to the promptness found in Japan, the bandai unlocked the door not a minute past 4pm, and about a dozen of us removed our shoes and entered the sento. I followed the women who gave the front counter bandai an afternoon greeting but strangely continued on ahead *without* paying. "They must be regular customers with some sort of membership," I thought, not giving it any more credence than that. I pulled out my four 100-yen coins and put them on the counter only to have the bandai push the coins back towards me with a smile. I stood there dumbfounded as my worst fears played out! Was he not going to let me in? My facial expression must have been the look of horror because I stood frozen not knowing what to do. He spoke to me in a low voice that I couldn't understand. He then got up from his chair, came around the counter and pointed to the calendar hanging on the wall behind me. Tapping his finger on the date, he found the words to say "free day – no charge" and immediately I felt relief. Maybe it was a day set aside for some community promotion? I don't think I'll ever know for sure, but I put the coins back into my pocket and made my entrance to the *datsuijo* (dressing area) for women.

Even though I wasn't proficient in the Japanese language, it was easy to be in tune with the level of comfort inside the sento. However stoic these women appeared while standing outside in line, inside they resembled a bunch of schoolgirls at a slumber party. Everyone was self-assured in choosing a locker. This seemed to indicate each woman had a "regular spot." I didn't want to be in the way, especially on my first visit, so to be considerate I carefully delayed my locker choice until they were sufficiently settled in. In Japan, politeness is displayed in the smallest of details and reaches far beyond the limits of language. Westerners can often be misinterpreted as rude, only because our mannerisms and customs regarding body language are in fact, different. There are more than 70 distinct gestures identified in Japan that are *not* used in the West; and as a foreigner, I knew I had some leeway, or a license to make mistakes. However, I didn't want to pull out my imaginary pass for this situation. I'm forever hoping that when I find myself in a state of true ignorance, my license to error will be accepted and my offense forgiven.

I was made to feel like one of the girls with exchanges of warm smiles, totally welcomed as we undressed in the small designated changing room. My neighborhood sento was clean and tidy and had what every sento needs – customers! As I got ready to bathe, I saw again the collection of flat fans called *uchiwa,* stored handle down in a clear glass vase. It was after my visit to the Asakusa sento I learned that this flat style fan in fact dates to the 17th century when they were popular souvenir items at major shrines. Today, not only is the uchiwa used at sento to cool off after a hot bath, but they're readily carried during the summer months, providing some relief to the intense jaw-dropping humidity in July and August. The uchiwa can also be spotted at restaurants that cook on *hibachi*-style grills, where the rapid fanning of hot charcoals is an essential technique for cooks. Most notably, the fan is always used where sweetly basted *unagi* (eel) is grilled and served. Cooked to perfection, the basted delicacy is served over a bed of premium white rice and eaten from a fancy lacquered box. It's incredibly delicious, consumed not only for taste but for its stamina-giving properties as well.

The floor in the dressing room at Manzai-yu was a spotless dark wood laid in four-inch planks. The clothes lockers were faced with a speckled, white laminate veneer, about the same vintage as the Asakusa sento. Very little inside this sento had been changed or updated over the past 30-years or more, so it too was in a strange time warp. The familiar, upright, army-tank-green metal scale stood solidly against the wall, this time under a tall ceiling of crackled white paint. I eyed different, colored, plastic rinsing bowls, half hardly stacked on shelves, the personal belongings of Manzai-yu's regular customers. All the bowls were stuffed with shampoos, soap, hairbrushes and towels. I thought about how this method of unsecured storage would never work in the United States.

Sadly, the taking of personal items only for the sake of taking is an all too common social defect, an unpleasant behavior linked to many social issues. But why was this different in Japan? In time, would it change? It wasn't only at sento I witnessed the amazing trust and respect for property. On many days I would see bicycles sitting unattended in front of the food market with baskets of shopping bags, backpacks and groceries left in the open, vulnerable to theft. Even in the underground parking garage at my apartment, a golf bag with a full set of clubs sat for months leaning against a wall. By far, the most surprising show of respect was the 200 yen (approximately $1.90 USD) in coin that sat on a chair seat at a bus stop, untouched for three days. Even with the hundreds of people who walk that street daily, the coin was left to be reclaimed by its rightful owner. Keep in mind, this is in the heart of the city!

The washing area at Manzai-yu had approximately 15 individual washing stations, all arranged in the same fashion as Asakusa with hot and cold *karan* (after the Dutch word kraan for faucet) mounted under a long, low hanging mirror. When I sat, the reflection of the mirrors gave the impression that this sento was larger than it really was. One noticeably unique characteristic was the spider leg vines that meandered across the high-arched wood ceiling. Thriving on a daily dose of steam, the plants somehow survived just like this sento.

In traditional sento construction that dates to the first half of the 20th century, a common feature is the hand-painted wall directly above the soaking tub. This open canvas usually incorporates Mt. Fuji in a seasonal theme. These murals seem to be a favorite topic of discussion by Japanese who want to tell me about their experience at sento, but at Manzai-yu, this was not the case. Instead a crude landscape was painted with a carnival scene in slightly garish colors. Due to the constant rise of steam, the painting was under a great deal of stress causing severe peeling and cracks all across the image. No doubt a nuisance when the paint chips fell into the water. I took my time that afternoon, soaking and washing, washing and soaking, alternating between the two tubs of very hot water. Listening to the chatter of the women made me feel like I was part of a secret girls' club, hidden away from the outside world. All in all, I was quite happy to celebrate Manzai-yu's humble heartbeat. That afternoon, I was quick to form the opinion that everyone must go to sento. Not only to make a connection with one's community, but because it truly was a place where one could enjoy stretching out in a large tub and soaking in revitalizing hot water.

I wished everything that seemed perfect that afternoon *really was*; but I'd been doing a fair amount of research on the public bathhouse, and the commentaries, official government numbers and future predictions of the traditional business were unsettling at best. According to the Tokyo Sento Association, if closures continued at the same rate, in less than 15-years, the sento we know today would be gone forever. Should this outcome be realized, I'm sure it would have negative implications on hundreds of communities throughout the country. Without sento, it's far less likely people will know their neighbors, contributing to a lifestyle of isolation that has a direct relationship to the rate of crime and violence. In addition, dreadfully at risk was the platform elders are given to sharing knowledge and teaching values to young adults. One might think printed media, television and the Internet can substitute or replace this loss, but I beg to differ.

Can sento survive? Well, *"it ain't the money; it's the money,"* an infamous family mantra coined by my father, who uses this seven-word phrase to make sense of sometimes senseless situations and many world decisions. I'm afraid this concept of how the world works applies to the circumstances facing sento. These small businesses, many of which are family owned, operate without any assistance or special funding from the government, even though a case could be made that some are near, national treasure status.

Since the early 1990's, The Sento Association has published a monthly, printed magazine (on line version at www.1010.or.jp) to help spread the word of sento and highlight individual success stories, especially when owners have raised their profits. Still, this hasn't stopped the decline. One popular and less aggressive effort to stay profitable has been through the addition of "pay for use" amenities like the hair dryer and massage chair. These small-coin options have helped, but far too unrealistic to believe they would be the driving force to keep a business solvent. Other recent changes include moving the bandai to a front counter position, updating the dressing areas and replacing the tile. In some cases, this has significantly improved business, but these makeovers require much larger investments. For most, this type of spending is far too costly. Every day sento owners struggle with ways to attract a younger clientèle, the seemingly most difficult challenge to secure the survival of the public bath.

The hot water at Manzai-yu had once again refreshed my body and recharged my mind. I got dressed so as to jump back into the fast track just on the other side of the wall. My curiosity to find more sento and discover the remaining nuggets was starting to take hold. What if I could do something to influence a positive change, a shift, if you will, away from the current decline? I wasn't exactly sure what I could do, but I would look for any opportunity to make a difference.

Chapter 7

California Cool

Just before moving to Japan, I was living in Manhattan Beach, California, a coastal community near the Los Angeles International Airport. I called home a rented, one-bedroom flat that was located behind one of the last remaining, South Bay, beach-side homes. Today, many of the 1930's, 1940's and 1950's style bungalows have been replaced with two and three-story monstrosities, appearing way too large for their lots, and sitting so close, a neighboring sneeze can be heard over the sound of the ocean waves. Where was the honor in saving the past? Well, as we all know, "It ain't the money, it's the money." Having lived in a place that survived the avid, southern California developers (and speculators) may have planted the first seed for my appreciation of vintage architecture. This fondness had now transcended to the older traditional sento, where fewer and fewer original buildings still stand as a testimony to the past. It seems the business of sento, with its unique structures, was undergoing the same pressures that face the remaining beach-side homes in California. I understand the process of destruction creates jobs, stimulates economies and makes us feel more modern, but is it worth it all the time?

Manhattan Beach is fabulous, due in part to sharing a stretch of pavement called *The Strand*, a pathway on the sand parallel with the Pacific Ocean. It follows the Santa Monica Bay coastline, stretching from Redondo Beach and north to Venice Beach. This extra wide sidewalk is filled (both day and night) with rollerbladers, bicyclists and people strolling on foot. It's a flat piece of heaven, and Manhattan Beach is smack in the center. For residents, the official bicycle is a chunky, thick-framed, two-wheeled transporter, sporting fat white-walled tires, cool paint jobs and simple mechanics - meaning no gears or hand brakes. Stopping is done the old fashioned way by reverse peddling. At the time, I considered myself a local and owned an ocean-blue cruiser fashioned with white Hawaiian flowers and an over-sized black vinyl seat. These beach bikes are built for slow, leisurely excursions on sunny afternoons with "no worries or hurries" in mind. In preparing for my move to Japan, it was one of the few things I decided to take with me and had it shipped by container with a few larger items. At the time I thought, "How cool it would be to bring a piece of the beach to Tokyo" having no real concept of inner, big city living. All I knew was I wouldn't be driving; so I figured the bike would give me one more mode of "easy" transportation. When it arrived, a Japanese friend helped me get it "street ready" by adding a basket, a license, a light and a bell.

Because my experience in getting to Asakusa had left me a little train-shy, I decided for the time being to take to the streets on my bike and search for new sento. I was *very* naïve to think that riding a bicycle in the city would be easy, especially a beach bike. Looking back at the sacrifices I made to look *California Cool* was really a bit too much. These bikes are ideal for long, flat, wide-open spaces, unlike anything I was encountering in Tokyo. In contrast to beach life, sudden stops and sharp turns in a mass of humanity are the norm. My inability to climb slopes and react quickly to surprise situations was down-right dangerous, not to mention that riding around on these fat tires felt very much like peddling in quick sand. Maintaining this "California image thing" proved to be quite difficult, but initially I wasn't ready or willing to abandon my original vision. I quickly learned to use the simple phrase *"sumi-masen"* (excuse me) and *"gomen-nasai"* (I'm sorry) while sharing the sidewalks with my fellow Tokyoites. The trade offs to the challenges were the frequent stares and out-of-the-blue comments like, "Nice bike" which, ok, I relished. For reasons I can't explain, because I really don't know why, my desire to look different in this man-made entanglement was strangely important. I didn't want to get lost in a crowd, so the extra attention only fueled my insistence to ride the big blue bomb.

In Tokyo, bicycles share the same path as pedestrians. This provides some increased safety from motorized vehicles; but without exaggeration, the sheer number of people on foot can be just as precarious. According to the Tokyo Metropolitan Government, the population density in Tokyo is 5,655 people per square kilometer. To help with the math, one kilometer equals 0.6 miles. That's a lot of people! In the popular shopping and business districts of Akihabara, Shinjuku, Harajuku, Shibuya and Ginza, more than 200 hundred people can cross the street during one green light, but even more mind-boggling are the intersections called "scrambles," where all 4 corners cross at that same time including in a diagonal direction. At a scramble, a pedestrian can easily be one of 400 people swiftly moving across the street in about 15 seconds.

Because most sento open around 4pm, I was usually on the street at the same time the graders were making their way home from school. It's an amazing sight to see children no older than 6 or 7 walk home managing the busy crossings and trains without an adult. Wearing their solid-colored hats, seemingly indifferent to the world, they head for home singing a quiet tune while their draw-string *bento* bag (lunch box in a sack) hangs from their square leather backpacks, swinging back and forth *in time*. These "little people" have no trouble asserting a polite aggressiveness required to make their way through the crowds of people twice their size.

I took to the street on bike and visited every sento I could reach within a 3-mile radius. Getting comfortable with the sidewalks and acquainted with the intersections was relatively easy. What proved to be the most challenging was the adjustment I had to make riding in an "opposite flow" of traffic. It was pure torture for my natural reactionary senses. One might wonder "Why?" Well, until you've vigorously peddled down a sidewalk and encountered peddling towards you a mother with two children on board is a full appreciation of "traffic flow" realized. Especially when you *both yield to the same direction* at 5 miles per hour! The simple fact is that when two cultures which have an entirely opposite modus operandi mix, watch out. In the United States, because the car, bicycle and foot traffic generally move forward from the right, I was a real moving hazard. Mindlessly I thought, I would automatically yield to the right - the absolute wrong way in Japan. The direction to which one yields is really an *automatic* sort of thing, based on years of living with people doing it the same way. It's just something one doesn't think about. These near collisions would happen often and were surely a highly frustrating experience for the less fortunate person sharing my path. I worked hard to switch off this embedded reaction, but my early days were filled with close calls. After a couple of months of "retraining," I finally fell into the natural practice of riding on the left and yielding to the left.

Despite this adjustment period, riding a bicycle gave me a great many pleasures. I rarely missed a beautiful garden that sometimes grabbed only a few feet of precious space, nor did I miss an exchange of smiles with the merchants and street cart vendors along the way. Bonus days occurred when I came across an *oden stand*, a Japanese hot soup eatery on wheels! Powering up with generators in the early evenings, these sidewalk and side-street eateries go through an amazing transformation. The cart is pulled to a location by foot or bicycle, and the owner sets up a full-fledged restaurant under a makeshift roof with soft plastic walls, lights, tables and chairs. To complete the scene, an admirable selection of frosty cold drinks and a delicious soup broth are served up with an assortment of seafood, vegetables and meat, all added at will. It was always a treat to find one. They are constantly on the move because of pressures that include disputes with the local police, merchants, and even with the *yakuza* (Japanese mafia) who try to control the street businesses operating on their turf. Nevertheless, my visual enjoyment was always enhanced by riding my bicycle and the informal friendships with merchants provided me an inclusive feeling among the hoards of so many nameless faces. In those early months, peddling on both the back streets and the major arteries like Hibiya dori, Daiichikeihin, and Aoyama dori improved my navigating capabilities and gave me a more intimate understanding of how the neighborhoods differed, something that could only be attained from a sidewalk view.

Using a map of sento locations provided by the city ward, I visited all nine operating in Minato-ku, methodically checking them off after each visit. What began as something to do while getting out and learning about the city started to take on a more serious purpose. I had scratched away enough of the surface to see how extraordinary these businesses really were. Like the many neighborhoods I visited, every sento was different – each with its own unique and individual personality. Some of the bathhouses in the ward had modern updates while others still operated in late-Taisho (1912-26) or pre-war Showa buildings, proudly intact with wood-heated boilers and towering stacks that billowed out smoke and ash in the late afternoons. A common theme among them all was the strong sense of community, evident at the moment of entry. Whether I was in *Koyama-yu*, the hard to find late-Taisho sento tucked away on a narrow dead-end street, or at the fully remodeled and modern *Tamagiku-yu*, where I was scolded for splashing a fellow bather, each one was a member of the sento family which provided that magical grounding effect.

Elizabeth Ann Ishiyama

Chapter 8

Bathhouse Architecture

On a visit to the Edo-Tokyo Open Air Museum I saw *Kodakara-yu* - a *sento* built in 1929 that had been moved to an 18-acre city-site for public display. It's a perfect example (inside and out) of a classic neighborhood sento built in early Showa. The danger of losing such buildings is starting to be recognized, so fortunately, Kodakara-yu has been saved from demolition and preserved for future generations to enjoy. In the film "Spirited Away" by acclaimed animator Hayao Miyazaki of Studio Ghibli, Kodakara-yu is the type of sento that gave inspiration for the "Gods' bathhouse" where a 10-year-old whiny and pessimistic child, Chihiro, finds employment after she becomes separated from her parents. Chihiro is a low-ranking bathhouse worker whose adventures are centered on the tasks required to keep the exotic visiting guests satisfied. Even though the animated interior and exterior of the bathhouse were exaggerated, the style of the barge board roof, called *Karahafu,* was not. It's the defining architectural detail strongly identified with older, more traditional sento. This design element was all the rage during Edo-period, and adopted again nearly one-hundred years later, as a sort of nostalgic fashion statement in architecture. It's my most loved exterior feature of sento buildings, so it was surprising to read in an art quarterly published in Japan that one of the country's most celebrated contemporary artists - Hiroshi Sugimoto stated he dislikes this chunky karahafu roof line. In fact, he was quoted as saying, "The thing I hate most about Edo-period architecture is the karahafu style…" The artist refused to use it in his design of the Go-oh Shrine constructed in 2002, rather opting for a style called *shindenzukuri,* developed in the fourth or fifth century in Japan. Maybe because so many Edo-period designs have been incorporated into contemporary styles, the architecture appears a little too "kitsch." At any rate, I'm not really sure why he feels this way, but for me, it remains one of my favorite design elements in all of Japanese framework.

Along with this identifiable roof line, one often finds *Tang gables* with corners that gracefully slope upward and dance with the sky. This architectural element is an example borrowed from China, brought to Japan after periodic dispatches of envoys during the 8th century. When these exchanges stopped, the "Japanization" of cultural assets began with further changes made to the borrowed styles, though origins of the designs are still quite traceable. Another crafty element sometimes found just under the eaves of the ash-gray tiles is one or all of the Seven Gods of Fortune. These cute, robust, folklore figures, six males and one female known as *shichifukujin*, are frequently seen together in a boat sailing the seas, spreading wealth, happiness and longevity. Individually, the Gods actually hail from a variety of religious faiths, including Buddhism and Taoism, as well as Japan's native Shintoism. The Kodakara bathhouse features the Seven Gods along the roof, and the museum brochure mentions that at the time this building was built, the original cost of the sculptures was as much as a new two-story building.

Other intriguing bathhouse design elements are the *gegyo*, a decorative wooden board used to cover the ends on a roof gable; the *rokuyou, a* decorative pattern formed in a beautiful shape on a gable pendant to conceal a nail-head; and of course the *hire* or *oni-ita*, a carved adornment mounted where the roof line peaks. I've taken literally hundreds of photographs of all three characteristics and from every angle imaginable. How this detail appears is often a "one of a kind," giving each building its beautiful and distinctive appearance.

Sadly, however, some sento in financial trouble have had to use make-shift materials and cheap labor to answer badly needed repairs. This includes exterior walls that have been covered up with concrete blocks or even an unthinkable inexpensive metal siding. The worst example of a building modification is the crudely constructed, coin-operated laundry facility. Usually the service room is attached to the entry, looking like an after thought with no regard to the final appearance. Adding the coin-operated washers and dryers which only grab a few daily coins, has been yet another way the bathhouse owners have attempted to raise their profits, but in doing so, have usually scarred the exterior facade creating an eyesore for the entire neighborhood. Sento in this condition look to be drawing their last breath.

In the Sento Association's annual directory advertisements for development assistance to build high-rise apartment complexes on sento properties can be readily found. Property developers target sento owners, tempting them with this changed business model by outlining a new, potentially promising proforma. If redevelopment occurs, the original building is always torn down and an apartment block takes its place. The sento owner becomes a landlord and sometimes exercises the option of continuing a smaller public bath facility on the ground floor. This has been the case for many sento I've visited, and since there are no official protections in place to save these historic buildings, more and more sento are being demolished every year.

In these last days of sento, when the daily receipts don't justify the operation, sento landowners are also opting to sell out *completely*, especially when the inner-city property is worth a sizable amount of money. So, it should be no surprise that when I find a sixty or seventy year-old bathhouse building, I would often stand in admiration, knowing it had not only survived the war, earthquakes and fires, but it was fighting the battle of its life.

After some tenacious effort, I finally made a breakthrough with the trains, allowing me to abandon my bicycle and reach out beyond my 3-mile neighborhood radius. With a handful of pre-paid train cards, I began using the tracks with my camera in tow, capturing the last examples of poured glass windows, solid wood trim, interior ceiling panels, and the many beautiful architectural adornments.

Chapter 9

Rapid Changes

Despite the rapid, western-leaning changes the country has adopted, one must keep in perspective that Japan emerged from its isolation and entered the world scene only at the end of the 19th century. Prior to this time, for the nearly 250-years under strict feudal rule, visitors of foreign decent were forbidden. This virtually stopped all outside influence except for a handful of special trade exceptions and considerations under precise articles outlined in the "Sakoku" Policy. The limited contact permitted outside trade with the British for a short time and then for a longer duration with the Dutch, Koreans and Chinese. The actual exchanges were made in a designated area near Nagasaki harbor and on a tiny island off the coast of Kyushu. In addition to the Southern trade, the indigenous Ainu people, who had a separate culture from Japanese, traded with the Shogunate via the Matsumae Domain on the Northern Island of Hokkaido. Apart from these insulated exceptions, Japanese people rarely communicated with, or, for that matter, even caught a glimpse of a foreigner. Likewise, the curious citizen who toyed with the idea of traveling outside Japan knew that if caught, the penalty was death. So the risk of venturing out beyond the confines of the country was rarely taken.

Many isolated attempts to end Japan's seclusion were made by expanding western powers during the 18th and 19th century. American, Russian and French ships all attempted to engage in relationship with Japan but were rejected. Only after the arrival of U.S. Commodore Perry with his black ships did Japan begin to seriously consider change. Beginning in the 1820s, American whaling vessels began working the seas around Japan to meet the rising demand for lubricants, lamp and candle oil back home. On July 8, 1853, Perry arrived in Kurihama near Yokohama and delivered a letter to the Shogunate to persuade Japan to change its closed door policy and allow American whalers to dock in Japanese ports for the re-supplying of their ships. This visit was the beginning of the end for the Shogun. It sparked a new, small collective voice that believed if they continued with their "closed door" policy, it would only agitate the United States (and other European nations), increasing the chances of an invasion. Information regarding the affairs of European colonization made its way back to the Japanese leaders heightening their concern for loosing autonomy. Japan never lacked fighting spirit, but because their weaponry didn't match the sophistication of the West, the difficult and painful decision was made to take steps towards working with foreigners. After an intense and historically interesting internal struggle, the decision to open the country helped preserve this precious autonomy.

In 1868, Japan embarked on a new great era of change defined in history as the Meiji Restoration, in which the country lost its Shogun, revised its foreign policy and adopted a more European-structured government. For the first time, Japan appointed a prime minister and established a newly defined role for the Emperor. During this period, despite the acceptance of or resistance to change, every aspect of Japanese society was affected, pushing the nation into competition with all the leading world powers. With open borders, Japan quickly modernized and worked cooperatively to expand trade with new countries, catching up at break neck speed. Fashion, architecture and entertainment were some of the first *visible* adaptations; yet amidst a complex metamorphose of modernization, some traditions faired better than others. Now, 150-years after the end of Meiji Restoration, the "old Japan" can still be found in a precious few cultural practices celebrated on a worldwide level. A face that is studied, emulated and branded as traditional Japanese. One only needs to look at the most recent "*Yokoso Japan*" (Japan Welcomes You) marketing campaign, a publicity effort that helps us understand the power of **brand**. Travel bureaus, billboards, websites and various other marketing outlets are being used to help travel agencies book foreign tourists using images of kimono-clad geisha, bonsai, kabuki theater, sushi, tea ceremony, festivals, sumo, cherry blossoms, shrines and temples as symbols that have become synonymous with the country. All used to entice the visitor seeking an exotic experience. "It ain't the money...it's the money stupid." Yet the public bath, which was born in Edo, endured through Meiji-period and stayed strong well into the 1960's, has never been a part of that *promotional brand.* It has remained out of view of foreigners and never attained the status of "traditional custom," something that might have changed its destiny.

Adding to the problem is Japan's under-thirty generation which does not view the public bath as a cultural treasure; therefore the forces of decline are coming fast and furious. It's just not *cool* to go to sento. For many, it represents a time in the not so distant past when Japanese were less modern and lacked many of the comforts the rest of the world enjoyed. Shinobu Machida, Japan's foremost expert on sento and the author of six books on the subject, writes, "The social side of going to a sento simply doesn't appeal to younger Japanese." Since the bath is now inside most every home in the city, the sento experience and tradition has been totally removed from entire generations, with a growing number of young adults who have never even stepped inside a neighborhood public bath. Young Japanese are striving to compete and maintain their acclaimed status as global trend setters; so there seems to be no regret in leaving this old fashioned practice behind. Those born after 1990 are moving faster than ever towards globalization, a term we hear tossed around almost daily, something, for that matter, the whole world seems to be rushing towards. This phenomenon, whether good or bad, is negatively impacting traditional culture on a world-wide scale. At the end of the day in Japan, the conscious effort to reject sento is probably the single most important reason why the small public bathhouse has no chance.

Within Japan's unique culture, there is the one prized tradition that is fighting back – and that's *sumo,* the Japanese sport of wrestling. It's a prime example of a time-honored tradition with roots firmly planted in Japanese history. It has taken extraordinary measures to maintain its popularity and protect its status. Historians agree that the origins of sumo date back 1500-years; however, it never really flourished as a spectator sport until the early 1600's.

Sumo was originally performed to entertain the *kami* (Gods) during *matsuri* (festivals), but has since evolved into entertainment for the masses. This ancient sport is perhaps the most exciting man-to-man match up of strength and technique in the world. A high-ranking wrestler demonstrates years of serious discipline by his steadfast dedication to endure the rigorous training required to compete. For the sumo fan, the analysis of skill and statistics is endless, with the drama centering on the thrill of victory and the agony of defeat. When outside influences began to chip away at traditional culture, the sport's association did not idly stand by; it instead took decisive action to expand the support base by including wrestlers from all over the world. Sumo coaches and stable owners (*oyakata*) now invite and recruit "outsiders" to participate and become full fledged members of the training stables. This change has significantly reduced its potential risk of decline and increased its supporters, reaching far beyond the boundaries of a nation. Asashoryu, Hakuho, Harumafuji, Kotooshu and Baruto, for example, are all top ranked and foreign born, not only earning a handsome living, but also endorsing products and appearing on a variety of Japanese television shows. In addition, they enjoy the adulation of hard-core Japanese fans, and I can comfortably say, to follow the sport is considered cool, even with its unbendable rituals closely tied to the venerable Shinto religion. Wrestlers from Mongolia, Korea, Estonia, Russia, China, Bulgaria, Georgia and others have mastered the language and fit right into a rigid hierarchy once only afforded to Japanese. I'm impressed that even with a history of strict adherence to tradition; "O sumo" has met the 21st century head on. The association has even gone so far as to take its top-ranked wrestlers to destinations like Las Vegas, Paris and Los Angeles for overseas exhibition tournaments, created to reach and entertain its foreign audience. This change has helped ensure the future of the sport by stamping the symbolic brand with bold persistence and spreading the excitement and interest to those who want to celebrate the age-old match-up of men.

Is it too late for sento? Well, I don't think we'll ever see the public bath as a part of the marketing campaign for *Yokoso Japan;* nor do I think it's realistic to hope that a generation listening to

Usher, Snoop Dogg, Cold Play and Alicia Keys will, any time soon, get behind a "save the Japanese sento" campaign. Since I started writing this book, more than 500 sento have closed in the 23 wards that make up central Tokyo. Maybe I should just feel fortunate that I am still able to enjoy the public bath in its twilight years and accept the fact I'm living in yet another era of change, where some traditions will just not survive.

Chapter 10

Ginza

In my continued search, I read a short, descriptive on line blog posted about a sento with a fabulous example of *kutani* ceramic tiles above the soaking tub. It was located in an area known as Ginza, the upscale shopping and entertainment district of Tokyo. The tile was from a remote village in the mountains in Ishikawa prefecture, a region of Japan that for centuries has exported beautiful decorative and functional ceramics to the world. The article cited kutani as being a true representative of Japanese craft. These historic kilns have long had a reputation of showcasing many fine quality artisans.

The sento, located in the upper blocks of Ginza, is one street off Chuo dori. It seemed to have all the ingredients of a preserved treasure in the center of a modern wonderland. I wanted to see yet another example of how Japan manages this "seamless marriage" of old and new. A sento in the middle of Ginza? The same Ginza where stores like Tiffany's, Mikimoto, Chanel, and Louis Vuitton all compete to attract the serious world shopper?

Oh yes - Ginza.

One only need to say the word and images of high fashion, fine restaurants, private hostess clubs and art galleries come to mind. Most famous for its nine blocks of upscale shopping, the district of Ginza has an appeal comparable to that of the Avenue des Champs Elysees in France, an over-the-top mecca of extravagance in Tokyo style. Shopping can easily dole out a strong dose of "sticker shock," but retail consumers are not alone. For years this section of the city has set records in land sales and lease prices, reaching heights that, to date, have been record-setting. Now, however, under a more tame economy, the real estate is more comparable to Manhattan, Zürich, London and Hong Kong. However, prior to the burst of the economic bubble in the early 1990's, the real estate in Ginza alone was valued higher than the entire state of California. I was surprised to learn a sento was located there; but what was even more surprising was the "Ah-ha" experience I had on that first visit. An epiphany, if you will, where my emotions and intellect came crashing together - with such clarity.

At the doorstep of 7-5, Ginza 8-chome, one will find oneself on the first floor of the Konparu building, hence the name *Konparu-yu,* an extremely modest sento located at the end of a long hall under the rise of office suites. Across the alleyway are the back entrances to the most sought after brands, including Burberry, the luxury mega retailer from the U.K. that made "plaid" an international fashion statement. Even in the midst of these modern day "big box" merchants, many more of the businesses in Ginza have a long and rich history, selling specialty products and offering services that can easily date to Edo. Their tiny entrances are barely noticeable on the backstreet's known to Tokyoites as the *real* Ginza. These established businesses boast generations of loyal customers, hidden away from the eyes of tourists who more often keep their stroll to the main street.

This part of the city is utterly remarkable on a weeknight, providing a sight few tourists, or, for that matter, very few Japanese ever see. In contrast to the modern western facade by day, Ginza at night is a place where the country's top executives and people of domestic influence are dined and entertained at the highest level. With similarities to a Thursday night (not so long ago) in the major financial districts of the world, deals are made, the finest wines are poured, and the cuisine is nearly unmatched. Uniquely Japanese, however, are the beautiful women, employed as professional hostesses in many of the areas clubs. This is *not* a red light district, rather a place where Japanese businessmen relax and finish an evening with colleagues with a bit more drink and sometimes a serious showing of karaoke in the company of the city's most beautiful women. These Asian beauties keep the ice cubes fresh and the whiskey-water full in a very "friendly" and professional manner. 30-minutes on either side of midnight, hoards of businessmen begin to appear on the sidewalks with women in beautiful dresses, evening gowns and an occasional kimono to partake in a curbside salutation.

This bowing and waving is a very public display of courtesy. After the many exchanges of appreciation, the women walk the men to their cabs and invite them to come back soon. After a final wave, the hostesses return to their club with memories and commissions of yet another evening. The cost of a few "after hours" in Ginza is not for the weak at heart - it can set one back hundreds or, more likely thousands of dollars, which is why this indulgent business caters only to a select group of the population.

Under the clear blue skies of October, I arrived at Konparu-yu late in the afternoon. For the lover of seasons, Tokyo in the fall is a real treat as the humidity subsides and the seasonal change in leaf color dazzles the eye. The sento was busy with mostly a steady stream of professional businessmen, dressed in dark suits and conservative ties. As they poured in I thought, "Maybe they're in Ginza for a business meeting, taking a quick soak before the long night ahead." Late night eating and drinking with clients is very much a welcomed duty for the executive in Japan, firmly part of the business culture; so maybe some had come to Konparu-yu as a form of "prep work." Or perhaps it was a needed break from the stress and strains brought on from their business day, a little time to unwind before going home. Whatever the reason, I wanted to believe the hot bath at sento was just the perfect place for Japan's modern society to keep itself in shape for any situation.

Once inside the sento, one would never know this was Ginza. The extreme glitz and swank outside was set against a simple and reserved interior located just behind a set of sliding wood doors. It was marvelous. The co-existence of traditional and non-traditional worlds that finds a balance was again so obvious at Konparu-yu. A *kamidana* (Shinto alter) was hanging on the far wall with a string of *O-shide* (zig-zagged folded paper) marking the sacred boundaries of the deity. In the same area a rambunctious variety show was on the television with lots of laughter generated from some of the country's top, guest talent comedians. The dressing room was small and the decor, like so many others, had seemingly gone unchanged for 40-years or more. How a sento could exist in this part of the city amazed me. As the glass door slid open to the washing and soaking area, I could see the impressive ceramic tiling on the back wall. Twelve large *koi* (carp fish) made a colorful palette of bright yellow, deep orange and jet-black, swimming above the two tubs.

Unexpectedly, a woman entered the dressing area wearing a beautiful, patterned silk kimono. Her mere presence created an even deeper time warp, as if I'd stepped back-in-time to Edo in 1765. She was maybe in her early 50's, and quite possibly working at one of the *ryotei* (Japanese haute cuisine) restaurants in the area. These kimonos are not worn for tourists, but are a respected cultural art form appreciated and enjoyed by many contemporary Japanese. Her hair was in a swirled bun and, as was the customary rule for women in traditional dress, she wore no jewelry. The kimono was carefully folded and left on the bench just before she went through the sliding glass door.

Together we started our personal washing routine, separated only by our thoughts, respecting each other's space with silence. Because Ginza is so over stimulating, the lack of conversation provided a perfect and precious balance. While examining the colorful tiles, I reflected on how both of us had come to relax and recharge our batteries inside these tranquil walls. Our hearts were baptized and our minds rejuvenated as we enjoyed the medicinal warm water. This sento was a modern glimpse into the past, playing out in such a way that really not much had changed in more than a century. Bathing at Konparu-yu is truly an Edo-period moment anyone living in the 21st century can experience, as long as the bath remains open.

I felt I'd come to understand *why* sento has survived all these years. Yes, the social benefits were incomparable, and the yin – yang balance to life's demands was paramount, but my epiphany occurred when I realized that equal in importance was the "void state of mind" one can achieve while soaking. This void is quite possibly similar to an abstract central concept found in the Buddhist philosophy, where "form is emptiness, and emptiness is indeed form." Identified as *shunya*, it's the core concept of the ancient teaching a Tibetan Buddhist spends a lifetime on a journey to achieve. On one's quest, the practitioner recites the *Heart Sutra* (a collection of aphorisms in the form of a manual) used as a pathway to the consciousness of this void state, a way, if you will, to reach a divine inner peace. It's my opinion that this state of emptiness can also be compared to the practice of prayer found in many world religions. In them, the internal or external chant of a formalized series of words lends itself as a vehicle for spiritual meditation. On that day, the hot water at Konparu-yu was my prayer, yet another reason why I'd come to cherish the public bath in Japan.

Elizabeth Ann Ishiyama

Chapter 11

Super Sento

From time to time, I exchanged rather lively conversations with Japanese women about going to sento. One such conversation occurred with a young woman in her twenties who was noticeably perplexed by my public bath enthusiasm. She turned up her nose when she asked, "Why sento?" I was the last person on earth she thought would go to the public bath. Generally speaking, most people who regularly frequent sento are either those born before 1940, families with small children or people residing in living spaces without a bath - like students who temporarily call home a simple sleeping flat near or on campus without a tub or shower. I didn't fall into these typical supporter profiles and because of my *non-native* status, my affection for sento was, let's say, a little odd. Well, why *did* I find this archaic business so interesting? I knew if I couldn't communicate my feelings correctly, I might be deemed a little eccentric, and, even worse, never win her over as a future patron of the public bath.

A question like this can't easily be answered in just one breath because the reasons are many. "It's not *just* about the bath," I said, "Going to sento is a slice of Japanese history in action, socially significant and amazingly rejuvenating. What strikes me the most is how fragile the business of sento has become; after nearly 400-years of existence, its days are numbered. Hundreds of locations have recently closed, and I want to see as many as I can before they all disappear. These visits also give me a sense of adventure, because I never know what I might find. The anticipation of encountering the unknown, the element of surprise is what makes it so much fun! And let me tell you, every bathhouse has something special to offer. It might be a pond with colorful koi, a meticulously maintained garden, or simply a variety of hydro-therapy tubs found at many of the remodeled locations. One of my favorites has a bath chair that emits a low voltage of electricity as one soaks. I know…mixing water and electricity sounds a bit creepy, but the electronic pulses that shoot through your muscles, creates this weird tingling sensation you've got to try!"

After my explanation, her nose turned down and I could see I'd managed to pique her sense of curiosity. As far as she could remember, she'd never been to sento; so I invited her to join me on a future visit; and then it came - the *big* question.

"Will we encounter a male bandai?" she asked.

"Well, yes, it's quite possible," I said, "but you never know until you go inside."

Later in the conversation she asked me, "Have you ever been to a *super* sento?"

"No," I replied. "What's a *super* sento?"

"It's a new concept bathhouse opening up in many areas of the city," she said, and then proceeded to fill me in on the details. From her description, it sounded more like a version of a *day spa*, but with a Japanese twist of large tatami covered relaxation rooms, and, of course – lots of food. **Japanese are serious about their food**. When I asked who goes to super sento, she thought they were popular with all ages and heard that business was booming. If I were going to better understand why sento numbers were dwindling, and *super* sento was booming, I needed to add this to my list of visits, and get a first hand look at the differences. For a nation of people who have a wonderful craze for hot water, I was pretty sure the super sento would be fun. With a few taps on the computer keyboard, the many super sento options in the greater Tokyo area appeared. One in particular, *Oedo Onsen Monogatari,* had just opened near my apartment; and the reviews were impressive with a special mention of its Edo-period theme interior and a customer count of more than 4000 on a weekend day. For comparison, the public bath in Tokyo is lucky to have 100 fee-paying bathers on a busy day.

Oedo Onsen was located on a reclaimed piece of land in Tokyo Bay, near O Daiba, a popular "destination location" for shopping, movies, first dates and dining. I'd get there by taking the *yurikamome* monorail, a driver-less people mover that travels over the beautiful, two-tier 798-foot Rainbow Bridge, connecting the relatively small island to Tokyo. Once over the bridge, one is provided with what I believe to be Tokyo's most captivating view looking back at the city. A painter couldn't create a more spectacular scene. The night-time composition is especially breathtaking with the hanging colored lanterns from tempura boats which slowly move like water bugs on the water. Dominant is a distant backdrop of countless illuminated windows floating in the dark from the multitude of high-rise buildings outfitted in glass, steel and concrete. In the center of it all, the brightly-lit Tokyo Tower reaches exactly 332.6 meters high (1091 feet) a lattice of steel built in 1958. It is the world's largest self-supporting steel structure, and the 20th tallest tower world-wide. The structure supports an antenna that broadcasts television and radio signals for important Japanese media outlets such as NHK, TBS and Fuji TV. The orange and white framework is a landmark for the city much like the Eiffel Tower for Paris, the Space Needle for Seattle or the Sky Tower for New Zealand.

I tried to set for this visit an open mind because, honestly, I felt a peculiar protectiveness about sento. The unappreciated business I'd come to know and love seemed threatened by a rival. Secretly, I feared that if super sento were just a bit *too super,* then going to the older neighborhood bathhouse might lose its appeal. Arriving at the onsen entrance, one passes though massive wood doors, fashioned with iron fittings similar to those found at the entrance of an Edo-period gate. My first impression was "Wow! So this is what would happen if Disneyland and Las Vegas had a baby." Surprised by the Hollywood-set-like presentation, my first impression was surprisingly positive. "This is going to be entertaining," I said to myself, and joined the admissions line that zigzagged much like a busy check-in counter at the airport. With a full staff of attendants, we moved quickly as an entrance fee of 3,500 yen ($32 USD) was collected. In return, we were given a map of the grounds, a locker key and an ID card to hang around our neck. My map printed in a large font read:

NOTICE

People with tattoos are not allowed entering.
People having tattoos will not get a refund if they
are forced to leave the building.

Forced to leave the building! What was this? I quickly felt relief
that my brief desire to get a tattoo while living in Oregon had not
materialized. What did tattoos have to do with this business? I was
encouraged to step up my pace and join everyone moving to the next
step.

Hanging on the wall were different patterned *yukata*, a simple
cotton kimono-like garment that's more casual than a kimono and
worn during the summer months or while staying at a hot springs
resort. In the early days of bathing, people in Japan wore a yukata,
then called a *yukatabira,* because the bath was more like a sauna and
the cotton provided protection from the hot steam. Today, with a
shortened name, yukata are still worn in public in a wide range of
designs and colors and are especially popular among young women
during *hanabi,* the impressive firework displays during summer.
Westerners have adopted a simplified version of the yukata, the
bathrobe, but wear it primarily as intimate apparel without the broad,
fancy ties and large cut sleeves.

Each super sento visitor picked from the dozen or so designs
which were to be worn inside the complex. After indicating I'd like
the pastel yellow one with the side-on portrait of an Edo-period
beauty, I made my way to the dressing area and slipped into the
comforts of my outfit. The dressing room was beautifully appointed,
contemporary yet still maintaining a classic traditional flavor. Rows
of highly-polished wood lockers were decorated with details from
well known ukiyo-e prints. My locker had the large tsunami wave,
one of the most widely recognized images by Katsushika Hokusai
(1760 – 1849) titled *Kanagawa Oki Nami Ura.* Hokusai was
considered a child prodigy and appeared in the spotlight among
fellow block print artists when he was only 15-years-old. Self-
proclaimed as completely obsessed with creating new designs, he is

said to have made the statement, "I live for nothing else," referring to his chosen art form. Hokusai gave the world a pictorial view of life in Edo with exquisite use of color, identifiable by his palette of warm earth tones, accented with deep orange, blue and green. By the end of his life, he was credited with producing over 30,000 different ukiyo-e images which today are real national treasures.

With a final check in the mirror, I proceeded to the public area where everyone was mingling barefoot in a painted Edo neighborhood setting. The street scene had painted storefronts and figures of townspeople dressed in styles of clothing worn 250-years ago. Cart vendors were selling food and a variety of simple carnival-type games were free for the children to play. It was fun to be among the vibrant props that replicated the streets of another era. To further enhance the atmosphere, a recorded chatter of merchants and street sounds played from carefully hidden speakers, bringing the set alive. By the looks of it, everyone was propelled back in time as they strolled around Oedo Onsen, enjoying their Edo fantasy.

Using my onsen map, I located the area where visitors make appointments for the optional spa treatments. The varieties of extras ranged in price from 3,000 yen to 7,000 yen ($28 to $65 USD) and were to be scheduled within the allotted 4-hour visiting time. If more than 4-hours are spent inside the complex, additional "over stay" charges are applied, a policy that encourages people to limit their stay, helping push the daily entrance total to a sizable number. Initially, I understood the restricted time limit because staying beyond 4-hours seemed like an easy thing to do. For an additional 15,000 yen ($135 USD), I booked a 30-point foot massage and a 70-minute Korean body scrub that had a warning attached discouraging booking by anyone with a "low tolerance" to pain. Hum, I was feeling pretty strong that day, so I ignored the warning and pre-paid my treatments. Before going to my first appointment, I would use the foot bath known as an *ashi-yu*.

Located outdoors, the open air bath was a man-made stream with a bed of small rocks cemented in place. The rising steam meandered across the grounds as the water flowed in the chilled air. Pulling my yukata up above my knees, I slowly walked in about 12-inches of warm water, carefully placing each foot on the variety of shapes. Where I began walking, the rocks were round and smooth, embedded low enough to feel outlandishly good. But as the stream swept around, the rocks gradually took a new demon-like shape, of 2-inch-high protrusions that were too painful to walk upon. I'd met my threshold of pain and surrendered by stepping out. I joined across the way a group of people sitting with their legs dangling in a round pool of yet another style of hot water. Sitting there put me in the middle of typical silent public behavior, something most everyone living in Japan does so well. In fact, breaking this social norm is noticeable. Compared to many cultures including my own, Japanese have one of the quietest public demeanors. However, this "day time" behavior can dramatically change after the sun goes down. For example salarymen can be spotted everywhere in the city after dinner, bumping shoulders with their buddies on the streets and sounding quite silly as their tone rises to a party level. Maybe I should coin a new phrase here…. "It ain't the alcohol…it's the alcohol!"

By 3pm the daytime calm provided everyone an uninterrupted front row seat to their personal thoughts. My mind wondered to the scheduled scrub treatment and that curious written warning. "Gosh, I hope I'd not miscalculated my strength." A brochure described the scrub as an ex-foliating process where a woman would hand rub my entire body front and back, head to toe, removing layers of dead skin. This would expose a new epidermis, a complexion glowing with freshness. Before I could discover how tough I really was, I'd first make a visit to the *zoku shin do*, a person trained in the oldest form of reflexology, to receive my "hands on" foot massage.

After an hour of successful pressure point discovery, I used my map to locate the bath area and proceeded to the women-only soaking room. This is the main purpose people dole out a fair amount of cash to come to Oedo onsen.

The wash area had the same familiar row of shower heads with individual hot-and-cold-water spouts, but also had a slight difference with dividing walls between each station. It was the same all important drill: Soap, rinse *and repeat*. On that Saturday afternoon, the soaking area was active with nearly 150 women and children, moving from one style of tub to another making every minute count. Unlike the simple rectangular soaking tubs at sento, Oedo Onsen had a much wider variety. The inventive choices were fun, with the most unusual being an elevated wood barrel large enough for three adults. In Edo, this type of tub was called a *kago-buro;* and once in the tub, one steamed the body by covering the tub with a lid woven from straw, shaped like a straw hat.

The main tub was massive, stretching nearly the entire wall with a posted sign that read, "Capacity 100!" At a glance, I saw the thermometer was at 41 Celsius, a tad lower than I expected. Having learned that 43 Celsius is 109.4 Fahrenheit, it seemed neighborhood sento water suited my newly reformed taste for "hot," so I wondered if this was going to be *hot enough.*

I tried all the soaking selections, including the outdoor space landscaped with rocks, trees and plants. This area is designed to imitate a natural hot-springs setting with bubbling water and natural elements under an open sky. It was the next best thing to an onsen located in the mountains near Mt. Fuji. At this lower water temperature, everyone is able to soak for a longer duration, so maybe the 41-degrees wasn't so bad after all. Off to one side, I could see the scrubbing room packed with bodies lined up side-by-side on stainless steel tables. Women outfitted in white, hospital-like uniforms were working intently on each naked body.

An hour later, a sturdy woman in her 50's appeared in the middle of the bath area, waved her hand and announced my name. I followed her back to the scrub room and was handed a small white towel. She instructed me to lie face up on one of the steel gray tables. The narrow metal surface reminded me of the same type tables used to transport and store dead bodies – yikes! She rolled up another towel, placed it under my knees and then proceeded to hose me off like a racehorse returning to the stable after a morning work out. My body was prepared for the scrub with a heavy application of a sandy cream that she rubbed on my arms, hands, legs, feet and torso. With only a small towel placed over my lower area, the whole process of applying the cream and scrubbing was done with a large loofa-type glove worn on one of her hands. I closed my eyes while she worked in long deliberate strokes, up and down, left and right and over every inch of my exposed body. The treatment of front and back scrubbing was repeated 3 times in all, which put me into a deep state of relaxation. When she finished, I was totally new, like a newborn baby.

I'd done it! My first super sento visit was complete. Totally satisfied with the experience, I was now familiar with the *"super"* in sento and understood how it compared to the more traditional bathhouse. As I returned to my street clothes I reflected that a recreational business like Oedo Onsen was not an alternative to sento, nor was it trying to be. Yes, they both had a common attraction centered around soaking in a communal setting, but that was as far as it went. A traditional sento was still a place to learn about meaningful local community issues, maintain a social dialog with neighbors, and practice a traditional form of culture which included a bandai. One could not compare traditional sento to super sento because that would be like trying to compare Belgian chocolate to German marzipan. You cannot - they are both deliciously sweet, yet totally different. You might prefer one taste over the other, but the lesson for me was that the neighborhood sento would not easily be replaced. More importantly, sento had *not* lost its appeal.

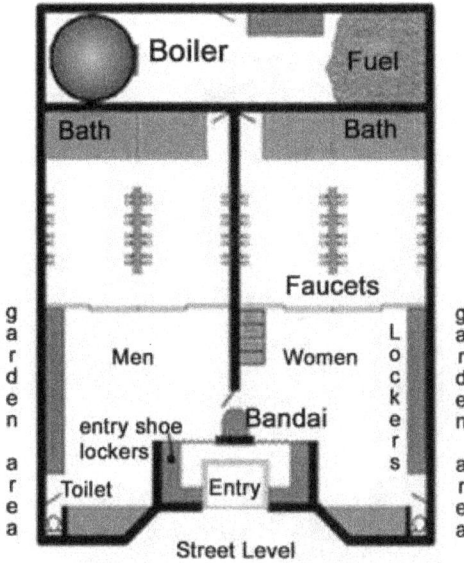

Typical Sento Floor Plan

Enjoy bath with manners

東京都公衆浴場業生活衛生同業組合

An example of a "bath manners" poster that can be found at sento locations visited by foreigners.

The character "yu" on a hanging noren in the entry of a sento open for business.

An example of a "bullet" chair dryer.

An example of shoe lockers with wooden keys
found at older and more traditional sento.

I often ran into this problem - here at Matsuno-yu,
my size 10 shoes didn't fit inside the shoe box.

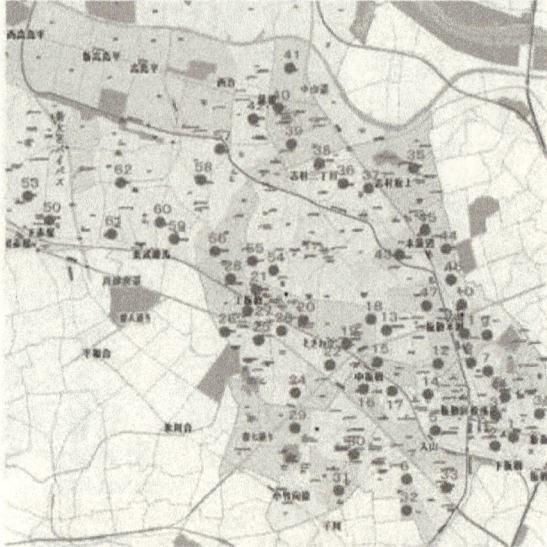

A snapshot of sento density within city limits.

One of Tokyo's finest at a koban near Gotanda.

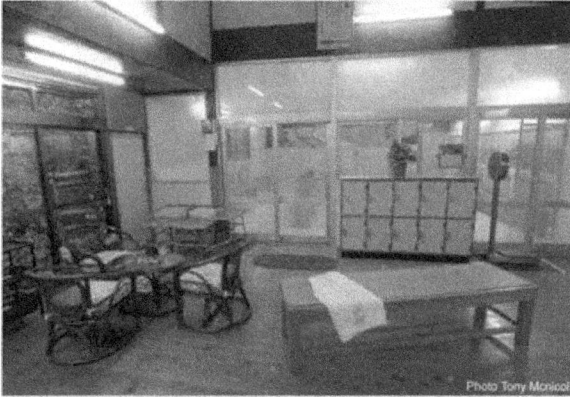

The dressing area of a 50-year old sento, with all the trimmings of a bathhouse interior, including a well maintained garden area to the left.

A view inside this washing and tub area is typical of a sento built in the 1950's. The extra tile feature running along the dividing wall (above the water faucets), is particuarily nice.

My California beach bike ready for the streets of Tokyo.

A very interesting Edo woodblock print illustrating a patron entering a sento with a seated bandai overlooking the large pile of New Year's gift money envelopes. Business was good.

A glass and chrome display of accessories for sale.

Like these at Yebisu-yu in Chigasaki, older and more traditional sento use baskets in the dressing areas instead of lockers.

A billowing stack one afternnoon in Kita-Senju.

Despite its run down appearance, this old cooler was in use inside the dressing area of a Tokyo sento.

Standing in front of a Fuji-san wall mural in Kodakara-yu.

Mural painter Toshimitsu Hayakawa sits for a break at a sento in Shitamachi. His paint cans, which once contained sardines and Pacific saury, now hold the colors that help him create majestic scenes of Mt. Fuji. In 2008, he is one of only 3 sento painters still working in Tokyo. During his career, he has witnessed nearly 5000 sento closures nationwide.

Ready to have an after dinner soak with my mother-in-law in Chigasaki.

Kutani tile in the entry of Asahi-yu in Chigasaki.

In this remodeled sento, the bandai has been moved to a front counter position.

Burning the midnight oil in Setagaya.

Komano-yu was rebuilt as an apartment building.

A detail from a screen at the Edo-Tokyo Museum, clearly depicting Edo period fireman with tattooed bodies.

A magnificiant rooftop detail on Umeno-yu.

Sakae-yu has maintained its fabulous architecture.

Well preserved traditional sento architecture

Sakae-yu roof tile detail

The rusted metal siding is masking many of this sento's needed repairs.

Where a sento once stood, an abandoned vending machine is left to rust.

Elizabeth Ann Ishiyama

The impressive architecture of Daikoku-yu in Kita-
Senju is by far one of the most beautiful in Tokyo.

Ebisu smiling under the eaves of Daikoku-yu .

Shinsake-yu in Ikebukuro with two anonymous
women who helped me find my way.

Yamaguchi-san stoking the boiler at Sakai-yu
in Ikebukuro.

Elizabeth Ann Ishiyama

Picking up emtpy milk bottles from Sakai-yu.

Yamaguchi-san's brother in the bandai box at
Sakai-yu during opening hours.

March 31, 2008 - After more than 50 years of business,
this was the last day the Azabu-juban sento would open.
Nearly 30 people lined up to soak for one last time. The
scrumptious tea-brown water was from a source located
50 meters below the building. This closure was a big loss,
not only for the local Japanese community, but also for
the large number of foreigners living in this neighborhood.
The "Juban" sento was one of the first sento I visited when
I arrived in Tokyo. Despite my smile, I was feeling quite
sad the city would loose this location.

Elizabeth Ann Ishiyama

Chapter 12

The Traditional Sento

Not long after I went to Oedo Onsen Monogatari, my craving for the more traditional sento really set in. So far, I'd completed nearly 30 different sento visits and found there was indeed a wide assortment. For me, the traditional style was always special, especially when the bathhouse building and interior dated 70-plus-years. It seemed these older and more classic locations were in the minority and often the most challenged to stay open.

I had two favorite oldies: *Takino-yu* (in the ancient city of Kamakura) and *Mitsukoshi-yu* (in Tokyo). These were two sento that provided a good *benchmark* for "the traditional;" however, Takino-yu was struggling and teetering on closure. The bandai said the owners had planned to close because the sento was running deep in the red, but members of Japan's Communist Party (JCP) had been campaigning for the local residents to return to the sento with a creative fund drive which had delayed the "lights out." The evening I visited, business was very slow. Obviously, it was on a slow death march.

In general, the word *Communist* is an unpopular word in the West. Unlike the United States where basically only a 2-party system is in force, Japan is represented by more than eight political parties, all of which make up the houses of the National Diet. The JCP is relatively small, with currently only 9 seats in the 480-seat House of Representatives; but still, they have a voice. The party adheres to the idea of a democratic revolution in order to achieve change in both politics and the economy. They tout a non-alliance position with other countries and work to complete the restoration of Japan's national sovereignty. Putting politics aside, I simply hoped the business of sento could remain a viable service in Japan, without assistance from the government or NGO, solely supported by its loyal customers. Hopefully, the Sento Association would put more focus on sharing secrets of success, giving the struggling sento owners an opportunity to discover more ways to tweak their business models to succeed.

Mitsukoshi-yu, another favorite oldie, was also fighting a slowing trend. Located in an upscale neighborhood of Tokyo, it was a large building in the Edo-period *karahafu* style, proudly standing on a busy street used to access the trendy area of Shirogane. Its presence was shared with storefronts that were a rare example of pre-war construction, many of which still had fading painted billboards that revealed their age. This neighborhood street had somehow survived the bombings of World War II, and the original facades had the adornments of businesses that had come and gone over the past century. To make way for modern-day car traffic, the sidewalk had been pushed up to the storefronts, leaving a narrow pathway wide enough for only two people to pass on foot, and like driving on a narrow bridge, passing had to be done with great care. Travelers on a bicycle or with a stroller must pull off to the side, stop and let the other person pass before moving on. A fellow American once described this neighborhood as a place that "captures the heart of a Westerner." He had lived nearby for years and, like myself, loved the twisted co-existence of the "old and new" Japan. When he walked home from work in the evenings, he passed the same hat shop that curiously never seemed to have a customer, and gave a friendly nod to the owner. On warm summer evenings, that same owner sat on his small, second-story balcony and sang traditional melodies while playing his *shamisen*, a centuries-old, 3-stringed instrument. These tunes could be heard within an earshot of his place and were enjoyed by those passing by on the street below.

Again, the elusive painted Mt. Fuji above the bath was not to be found at Mitsukoshi-yu. Rather, a large mural in tile of a woman with flowing brown hair spanned the back wall. With the exception of the outdoor museum, I'd *yet to see* a painting of Mt. Fuji at sento, and started to think this was a rumor spread among people who never actually go! However, in this case, I couldn't help but notice that the woman depicted in the tile had a strong resemblance to the woman bandai on duty. She told me she'd been the owner of

Mitsukoshi-yu for 25-years, and had recently decided it was time for the sento to undergo an extensive remodel in hopes of injecting some new life into the business. Starting that following month while the construction work was under way, the sento would be temporarily closed.

"So who comes to sento?" I'd asked, and most importantly "When and why?"

She replied that her customers were generally split down the middle in terms of men and woman, young and old, with peak times at 5pm and 9pm. It was her opinion that almost everyone who came to wash and soak did indeed have modern plumbing and baths at home, but because of the social benefits, they came to visit with neighbors and friends.

"Who was the woman over the tub?" She just smiled and said, "Oh, it's not really anyone."

Starting that April, the construction work required to give this sento a face lift would begin and was expected to last well into the new year. When asked if the roof and its stained glass window facing the street would stay intact, she said they had plans to keep portions of the exterior, but not all the changes had been decided. My hope was that it wouldn't change too much. It was getting harder and harder to find a sento in the city that hadn't been gobbled up by an apartment complex, or worse yet, completely replaced with another business. In the months to follow, each time I passed Mitsukoshi-yu, I couldn't see any visible changes from the street and wondered what was happening inside.

Chapter 13

Tattoos and the Bath

After being handed the flyer at Oedo Onsen *forbidding tattoos*, I wanted to understand the reasoning behind this message that warned of being "86'd" without a refund. Were tattoos also strictly forbidden at sento? To help answer this question and make sense of the policy, I researched tattoo in Japan.

Apparently the earliest mention of *horimono* (tattooing) is in the third-century Chinese text titled "The Wei Chronicles," where the indigenous Japanese (Ainu) are described by the following passage:

> *"Men, young and old, all tattoo their faces and decorate their bodies with designs..."*

For the *Ainu,* tattoos firmly belonged to the realms of religion and magic. The women were tattooed at the time of their wedding with an upward twirled "mustache" along with different abstract geometrical designs applied on their arms and legs, the implication being that the arms and hands work for the husband while the lips must speak for him. Hard evidence of tattooing in Japan was found in the excavation of a large tumulus mound near Osaka in 1977. It contained two *haniwa* (clay images), dating to the 5th century indicating faces with clear depictions of tattooing. Moreover, research by Helen Burxton tells us that during the 17th century, tattoos were a way in which society kept track of its criminals. If a person was found guilty of a third offense in Chikuzen (Northern Kyushu) for example, the forehead of the perpetrator was tattooed with the character for *inu* (dog), while in Satsuma, a circle was tattooed near the left shoulder. In similar times, a double bar was imprinted on the upper arm in Kyoto, and in the ancient city of Nara, a double line encircled the bicep of the right arm to identify the offender. One could summarize that this historical practice began the association of tattoo with certain fringes of society.

Later in *Edo,* artistic tattooing known as *irebokuro* emerged. The word is comprised of *ire* or *ireru,* meaning "to insert," and *bokuro* or *hokuro* representing a "beauty spot." These early beginnings took the form of a series of dots and were less pictorial. According to historian Tamabayashi Haruo, a select group of specialty tradespeople started using their bodies as "a canvas" for what later became elaborate and beautifully detailed designs. It's important to mention that within these diverse trades folk, a great range of classes existed; so it cannot be simply stated that acceptance or practice was widespread throughout every rank and file. To illustrate these differences, we can find in the 1936 book *Bunshin Hyakushi (A Hundred Styles of Tattooing)* the author making reference to a few lower-ranked courtesans who tattooed themselves with the name of their favorite customer. These tattoos, however, could be the cause of trouble if the woman had several different loyal customers; and the book sites that some women repeatedly tattooed over old names whenever their best customers changed. In contrast, however, Cecilia Segawa Seigle writes in *The Glittering World of the Japanese Courtesan* that tattooing was considered inelegant and indiscreet among high-ranking geisha, and as such, was a practice to be most avoided.

Under the absolute power of the Shogun, the strong command brought two and a half centuries of peace and stability, providing an environment that allowed for culture to develop and mature. Such cultivation gave people of Edo a variety of options not only in food and entertainment but also in personal fashion. Choices made were driven by a strong sense of what was called *iki* - a term in English that might translate as "ultra cool." Iki symbolized the nature of style, culture and spirit in Edo, influencing many things. Among select groups, tattoo was iki. The fire fighters for example, took this level of artistic expression by displaying very elaborate tattoo designs on portions of their bodies. A popular motif was koi swimming upstream on their backs which represented a potent symbol of strength and bravery. This design was thought to provide protection from the dangers of fighting fire in the predominantly wooden city. Generally speaking, however, wealthy, upper-class merchants, the majority of townspeople and gainfully employed samurai did not participate in this form of artistic expression. This art form experienced a golden era, achieving the peak of its popularity during the Bunka Bunsei-period (1804-1829) when a number of professional tattoo artists began to appear with infamous reputations.

After 1867 the ruling classes of Meiji-period who were never happy with the practice, succeeded in persuading the Japanese government to pass a revised and more explicate law *banning tattooing*. During its prohibited years, Japanese tattooing was kept alive underground, automatically attracting new fringes of Japanese society, including professional gamblers and the *yakuza* (Japanese mafia). The yakuza became notoriously famous with their elaborate, large tattoos. As a result, the art form has strongly maintained its identification with the highly organized (and sometimes dangerous) crime faction. The origin of the yakuza is a matter of debate. There are some early traces to the Tokugawa era. This is when the country had ruling clans that were given limited power by the Shogun in defined geographical areas. Taking power away from certain clans and shifting areas of rule was one tactic the Shogun used to balance and retain his power. When a power shift took place, sometimes a clan was stripped of its status, which resulted in many samurai loosing their employment and livelihood. It's estimated that as many as 300,000 unemployed samurai became leaderless men known as *ronin* during this period. Many ronin joined the merchant class, but some were forced to accept less than honorable ways of support. It was in defense against these wandering men that servants of the town created gang-like protection services, many of which were regular townsfolk who stood up in defense against the sometimes destructive outlaws. It's believed that some of the protectors then formed tightly-knit gangs that were the predecessors of the modern-day yakuza. To display their allegiance to the group, these members began to practice the art of tattooing their bodies. But as history goes, there's always a lot of "gray" – or truth beyond the obvious black and white facts, because even some unemployed ronin formed protection services so the theories of the origin of yakuza are **very mixed**.

In the world of tattoo, nothing can compare to Japanese yakuza body art known as *irezumi*, which, on occasion, covers nearly the entire body, including the buttocks. Naked, a fully-tattooed yakuza body looks like it's clad in colorful, long underwear, intricately patterned with a variety of dragons, flowers, deities, tigers, mythological creatures or warrior heroes. Although one cannot generalize, Helena Burton of Oxford University who spent a full year studying Japanese tattoos, cites Jacob Raz, who lived with and researched the yakuza for several years, as describing tattooing within the yakuza as a symbolic costume. Raz gives four reasons why a member of the yakuza chooses to be tattooed: (1) to pass an initiation rite to enter the order; (2) as proof of perseverance and manliness (going through the painful process of tattooing); (3) to symbolize the irreversibly of entering the world of the yakuza; (4) to bear on one's body (preferably with pride) the trademark of the order. Today, the number of the yakuza members with full-body tattoos is thought to be decreasing, although devoting one's life to the organization is still the way to survive. As one rises in rank, the member usually becomes more discreet, showing his allegiance in ways that are less detectable.

I need to make it clear that in many wonderful downtown neighborhoods in Tokyo, **tattoos and sento do mix**. This has been confirmed to me by credible people, born and raised in the downtown borough and quite familiar with sento culture. Unlike the operators at an onsen spa or traditional mountain hot-springs retreat, sento generally owners know their customers. It's inside these community walls one finds tolerance and the understanding that the world is comprised of many social classes, trades and guilds, making up the whole of society. Sento is a place where many social classes have always mixed and continue to mix in a truly cooperative and sociable manner.

After living in Japan for only a short while, I'm aware of the increasing number of artistic lifestyle tattoos on young Japanese adults (both boys and girls), who are without question, **breaking the stereotype of this art form and its association with the mafia**. As the world becomes smaller, new global superstars in music and sports are being created, and in a form of admiration, fans copy their style – *including the art of tattoo*. I can quickly put a list of names together of entertainers and athletes from around the world who have risen to idol status, and nearly all of them have a tattoo. This translates yet again to the pending arrival of new societal changes for Japan, which I imagine will lead to relaxing the ban of tattoos at the onsen in a matter of only a generation or two.

Elizabeth Ann Ishiyama

Chapter 14

The Boiler Man from Ikebukuro

My outings to find *sento* afforded me the chance to taste all the wonderful types of neighborhoods in Tokyo. On one afternoon I decided to go to Ikebukuro with the goal of being the first in line to soak, something all serious lovers of hot water want on occasion. Ikebukuro has a large commercial district and is a major commuter hub with the second busiest station in Tokyo. It's well known for its karate *dojo's*, hard working people and a large number of sento still open for business. I love Ikebukuro, mostly because of the people with their "no nonsense" edge, prevalent in real working-class neighborhoods. Ikebukuro could be compared to a middle-America blue collar neighborhood where hard work, honesty and community are all qualities held in high regard. "*I is what I is,*" as Popeye used to say, and Ikebukuro runs deep with a no frills way of approaching life.

As usual I exited the station and set off on foot, looking for clues to a bathhouse. Sometimes I joked about being able to "smell" a nearby sento, and if my nose wasn't properly working, I stopped at the corner *koban*, a community "police box," occupied with one or more uniformed officers. Every koban has a large map of the neighborhood with a friendly policeman and a will to help. There are hundreds of "police boxes" throughout the city, and they function as the eyes and ears at street level, serving each neighborhood with real community policing. On that afternoon, I'd wondered off into a neighborhood that looked just perfect for sento. The only problem was that after 30-minutes of walking, I hadn't found a bathhouse. Neither a sento nor a koban was in sight. I resorted to keeping an eye out for older men and women walking down the street with their personal rinse bowls in hand, stuffed with the accouterments for an afternoon in the bathhouse. This sure-fire clue always put me on the right track, and on two previous occasions, that exact scene played out. Like a lost puppy dog, I had followed behind as if I knew all along where it was I was going! The worse case scenario meant I had to ask a person at random if he or she had any idea where the sento was, and too many times to count, I was led (almost hand in hand) right to the front door. I always felt bad about taking someone's time, but it seemed everyone was positively pleased to assist. Using it as my last resort, I singled out two women walking in my direction, and they responded in the same overly polite way. All too anxious to lend a helping hand, we marched down the street together, around a few corners and deep into the backstreet's of the neighborhood.

Soon we arrived in front of the most perfectly intact, late Taisho-period sento, reflecting the aura and grace of the past. I jumped up and down in delight, which I'm sure made them wonder why I was displaying such odd behavior. Unfortunately, everything was locked up with no signs of life; so I wasn't sure if we were too early, or *years too late*. From the exterior, it looked completely original, just as I imagined it did the very first day it opened. Right in front of the sento, nearly blocking the front entrance, was a very large boulder, almost three feet high and four feet wide. "It sure was in a strange place for a rock of its size" I thought, maybe an old landmark with some historical importance, or possibly marking an ancient territorial dividing line. I had no idea, it just looked very out of place. In short order, I was motioned to follow both women again, and they led the way down and around another winding street. In less than 10 minutes, we were standing in front of another public bathhouse, this one on the ground floor of a fairly new brick apartment building. It was still in business because a milkman had just unlocked the metal partition and raised it high enough to crouch under to make his delivery. Using a bicycle equipped with a cart, it was his job to pick up the empty flavored milk bottles, and restock the business with a fresh assortment. It was then I realized that the "slowing business of sento" was also being felt by people who were providing goods and services to this fragile trade. I took a few pictures of the milkman and thanked the women for their wonderful assistance. Like the many nameless people before them, they disappeared into the streets, deservingly content with their work as extraordinarily polite, short-term ambassadors of Japan.

I had just about an hour before the sento opened, so to pass the time, I walked up the street and went inside a western style diner. Too late for lunch, and too early for dinner, I ordered a coffee and a desert from a woman who introduced herself as Ms. Mari Kobayashi, the owner of the diner. I did my best to explain why I was in her neighborhood and a delightful conversation ensued. She surprised me with an announcement that she knew the owner of the sento and would give him a call to try and arrange a meeting before it opened. What luck - this would be a jackpot visit! She made the phone call and instructed me to go back to the sento under the apartment building and find Yamaguchi-san working the boiler just beyond the side gate. Wonderful - a chance to see how the hot water is prepared! It had started to rain again, and in keeping with the local code of courtesy, Kobayashi-san lent me her umbrella, and off I went ready to have a behind the scenes look at the public bath.

Yamaguchi-san was quick to greet and enthusiastically showed me the boiler room, the heart of sento. Stacked from floor to ceiling were long boards and short boards and broken-down palettes all shoved tightly together like the inside of a beaver's den. There was hardly enough room for two, and a small overhead bulb gave off just enough light to reveal how he cut the wood to feed the roaring beast. His tall, lanky stature "man-handled" the electric saw, as he sliced through the scrap wood that had been collected from around the city. Amidst the shrill of the blade, pieces approximately twelve inches in length were cut and thrown into the flames. The ease with which he posed for me while slicing chunks of wood mimicked an experienced fashion model on a location photo shoot. The more wood he threw, the more intense the fire became and the louder the roar when he opened the hinged door. The towering chimney must have been pouring out black smoke as we laughed with each picture I took. The boiler box had become so hot, my camera lens had a difficult time dealing with the fierce bright glow each time he tossed wood into the waist-high compartment. I could feel the heat as the flame spit sparks of burning wood to the dirt floor at our feet. He stoked the fire with a jumbo smile that gave me the impression he truly enjoyed this part of his day.

Yamaguchi-san believed that only approximately 25% of the remaining sento in Tokyo still used wood-burning boilers. Most had fully converted to oil, but he was a traditionalist and I could see he liked it that way. He and his brother had each inherited a sento business from their father, and with great pride, they carried on a family tradition. We were feeding the fire that would heat the water at *Sakai-yu* operated by his brother, and as soon as the water reached a scrumptious 43-degrees, he would repeat this same process at Shinsake-yu, the sento with the large rock. This is where Yamaguchi-san would also occupy the bandai post until close. I inquired about the massive boulder in front of his bathhouse, and was told it was his father who loved that rock, ordering it to be left standing in its original place after he had the sento built. Japanese love symbolism, and quite possibly this rock now symbolized their father's love for the neighborhood, his passion for sento and the dedication he had in serving this community. He had successfully passed these traits on to his sons who worked very hard at keeping a Japanese tradition alive.

A day in the life at sento

For a business that is typically open 6 days a week, the Yamaguchi's kept a schedule that closely resembles the following:

13:00 – 14:00 Prepare the boiler, heat the water and fill the tubs.

14:00 – 15:30 Turn on the lights, prepare the till, restock/order goods for sale and perform general maintenance, including care of a garden or the grounds.

16:00 - Unlock the door, hang the noren and greet the customers.

23:30 – 01:00 Lock the door, drain the tubs, scrub the tiles, sweep and clean the dressing area, clean the

                    toilets, wash down the floors, clean the rinse
                    bowls and tidy up.
01:30 -   Call it a day.

Long days and physical work are offset by the gratification of bringing a magnificent tranquility to the neighborhood. Inside the world of sento, the urban clamor vanishes, and as long as there were customers, the work days would pass with ease.

Elizabeth Ann Ishiyama

Chapter 15

Three Short Stories

I
Deep in the Hood

Tokyo emerged in the last half of the 20th century as a world-class city. It not only supports *but demands* a wide selection of fine cuisine, readily available at all price levels. An intense competitive nature drives Japanese chefs to emulate exquisite examples of edible fare from every corner of the world. In return, an unmatched appreciation continues to feed this quest for excellence. No matter how critical one may be regarding the Michelin restaurant rating system and how its coveted stars are awarded, one can't disregard Tokyo's achievement in 2007 in acquiring nearly more stars than Paris, New York and London combined. Everything about food in Tokyo exceeds expectations; and when it comes to sushi, Japan is I must say, impossible to surpass. The availability of fresh sea life from its markets allows for the highest of standards that even the most easy-going salaryman adheres to. Sushi is where Japan puts its best foot forward, and in the city ward of Minato, *O Kame* sushi is one of hundreds of treasured establishments, pleasing even the pickiest bon vivant. Under the skillful guidance of a competent chef and owner, O Kame can bring a smile to any lover of the Edo-style sushi. It was at this restaurant I met a fellow diner who told me about the *sento* he went to as a child. His face warmed as he remembered his neighborhood public bath in Kita-Senju, where he believed the sento had a 400-year-old history. He had my full attention as I'd been searching for a sento that was still open with such a past. The sushi chef retrieved a map, and made a copy of the area neighborhood, pin-pointing the suburb located across the Arakawa River. During Edo-period, this area was the "stopover place" for

103

visitors and newly arriving residents traveling to the city of Edo. It had long been considered the gateway to the capital city. I couldn't resist changing my plans for the next day and go find this historic prize.

Kita-Senju is a suburb of Tokyo, geographically due north of the Emperor's Palace. If one wants to get up close and personal with the people who make this city "happen," along with the friendliest merchants in all of the greater-Tokyo area, then head straight for Kita-Senju. The area has no shortage of pachinko parlors, and features a precious historic main street preserved with storefronts dating to Meiji-Period. Kita-senju is, what we say in the United States, "small-town friendly." Warmth and congeniality radiate from the people who reside in these parts, even the young teenage street boys seen hanging around with their shaved eyebrows and dyed hair are as courteous as the merchants who smile and invite travelers off the streets to join them for cup of *matcha* (green tea) and traditional bean curd confectioneries.

It's a stretch too far from the noted sites visited by foreign tourists, so Kita-Senju makes a foreigner feel, well...*quite foreign.* Sometimes for self-amusement when I walked down a street outside the city core, I had fun playing a little street game. After passing a person, I'd quickly turn around and find this person had *also turned,* staring in wonderment at my presence. Their facial expression of inquisitiveness was always impossible to mask, and it gave me a laugh. This wasn't so easy to do where I lived because according to the 2007 numbers, 22,092 registered foreigners were among the 196,318 residents that made up the Minato ward, making it far more common to see someone of non-Asian descent. No surprise since Minato is home to most of the foreign embassies as well as many global corporations, foreign institutions and some of the world's largest International financial firms. As I walked down the street of Kita-Senju, I knew this part of the city was where I could play "caught ya' looking," but there was no time for that, because my purpose was to find the sento with the rumored 400-year-old history. Once past the historic main street, I had to go a little further north across the river; so I hailed a cab, showed the driver the spot on my map and hoped for the best.

Once across the bridge, the buildings became even lower, in most cases reaching no higher than three stories. The driver did not appear to have a strong grasp of the area because he kept pulling off to the side of the road and referring to the map. "What would this sento look like?" I thought, as the taxi pulled to the curb for a *fourth time*. We circled twice around the same block, and the driver told me to get out. "Here? But where's the sento?" He was in no mood to help me further, so I paid him my fare and stood standing at the edge of an empty parking lot. I waved to a woman coming out of a small warehouse and we met in the middle of the street. I asked, "Where's the sento?" She pointed to the empty parking lot behind me, and crossed her hands in the shape of an "X," a gesture used by Japanese to indicate closed. I then saw the old and rusty cold-drink dispenser standing alone like a ghost at the curb, surely a leftover from the days when the sento was open. My dream of finding a 400-year-old sento was crushed. This sento had not survived. This sento was gone.

II
Gotanda

Updates and changes made to a sento interior range from fixture updates and tile replacement to a complete revamping of the floor plan, whereby the bandai is moved out of the bathing area and placed behind a counter at the front entry. These changes give each sento a unique style and a first impression surprise that makes every new visit fun. Far from the franchised businesses of today where most follow a cookie-cutter concept, going to sento is like visiting a personal home. It's impossible to find two exactly alike. Intellectually and emotionally, big changes to sento were sometimes disappointing; however it was my visit to *Manpuku-yu* in Gotanda that gave me the power to see change from a slightly different angle.

Just a couple of blocks from the JR station, the entry to Manpuku-yu is located under large neon kanji characters that spread a warm pink glow over the sidewalk in the evening. The first thing I noticed when I entered was the size! Large is an understatement - it was the roomiest public bath I'd ever seen. The bandai who collected my coins sat behind a set of dark green shutters that made it difficult to see his face. Was that supposed to make me feel more comfortable with a male bandai? The fact I couldn't see his face bothered me more. I was a bit more at ease when I spotted the coin-fed hair-drying chair, sitting alongside the low-benches covered in an imitation tatami. Funny how that bullet chair made me feel so *natsukashi*, a Japanese term used to express a warm and fuzzy feeling one gets when seeing something familiar from the past. The big surprise on this visit, however, was the dozens of updates that were all piece-mealed together, which in design terms, had absolutely no cohesiveness. Perhaps many of the materials were chosen because of their cost effectiveness; nevertheless, the disjointed appearance was quite unexpected, even bizarre. The visual twist from the multitude of different types of tile in the washing area was not to be outdone by a photographic mural of birch trees, under a multi-colored striped ceiling that looked like a circus tent! The collection of colors and patterns swirled in an atmosphere of whimsical playfulness. Over time and with regular use, tiles inside a sento need to be replaced. At Manpuku-yu, this replacement process had taken an unusual turn. Old tiling was left to lay right beside newer tiles. On the floor, on the wall trim, in the tub, on the wash stations, everywhere one saw tile. There was a kaleidoscope of color and patterns that unfolded its past in just one glance. The myriad of blue, yellow, red, brown, gold, beige, and green were all fixed in a haphazard way of repair and replacement which made a sort of living history of time lines through color. Some tiles were solid, while others were patterned and fixed in such a way that the random layout created an unrepeatable scheme, something that could only be achieved by years of a piece-by-piece process of labor. Nothing matched. But did it matter? The fact that this sento was open for business and serving the neighborhood was far more important than whether it would ever make the cover of Architectural Digest Magazine. Manpuku-yu's interior was the *real deal* - a living time capsule right out of the groovy 1970's. It reminded me of how today's fashion industry reinvents itself by grabbing inspiration from the 1960's and '70's, in everything from clothes to furniture. The "retro" look has helped create popular marketing campaigns for many retailers looking to touch our nostalgic hearts. In the same vein, Manpuku-yu was *retro chic* without even trying! Its visual transformation had stamped its impression on me, giving me a deeper appreciation for the extreme differences one can find inside the public bath.

My passion to encounter more unexpected gems was equal to my desire to find sento that were more traditional and classic. This sento was a good example of how today's bathhouses did not need to *fix itself* in the past, rather an absolutely perfect case in point of Japan's flexibility to incorporate modern changes and make *it work* with the past.

III
The Shimizu-yu Kitty

Since I'd graduated to "having no fear of trains" (well – almost), the instant access to the city's neighborhoods surprisingly made this overwhelmingly large metropolitan area feel rather cozy. And in this strange comfort, I gladly took my proper place in Japan's complex society and became one of the millions of people who daily demonstrate to the world how a mass of people can move from one location to another with such ease. The trains and stations are all nearly spotless, and the strict adherence to the precise timetables makes using the rail a dependable mode of transportation. From the speed and comfort of the *Shinkansen* (bullet train), to the privately owned outpost lines, the efficiency is outstanding.

The train system is comprised of more than 22,000 miles of above ground rail routes, and hundreds more located underground. Despite the millions of people who ride the train every day, Tokyo has made great strides in adding additional lines that have remarkably decreased the "rush hour crunch." The white glove touting rail employee pushing people into a commuter car like a human sardine can has been virtually non-existent for more than 25-years. Don't let me mislead you, finding a seat at rush hour on a line that reaches the outer suburbs of Tokyo can still be difficult, but commuting in this fashion has much improved. The number of choices one has to get from point A to point B has increased, bringing relief to morning and evening peak travel times. The train had finally become my gateway to finding new sento, despite the mistakes I still made. Even with my navigational handicap, the extra effort always paid off because just steps away from the many hundreds of stations were undiscovered jewels of the bath.

On a Sunday afternoon in April, I exited the Tokyu-Meguro Line, a small private rail line in the thick of the Musashi-Koyama neighborhood, and found *Shimizu-yu*, by far the busiest sento I'd seen. The weather was rapidly moving from spring to summer and the days were getting warmer. The mercury was pushing 25-degrees and the humidity was starting to show itself. When it's cold in Japan, going to sento lubricates the joints and relaxes the muscles, but as the weather changes to summer, soaking washes away the grit and grime that sticks to your skin in the humid city air. In April, soaking at sento can offer relief from both seasonal extremes.

Shimizu-yu was a bathhouse that dated from Taisho 11 (1923) and was renovated in Showa 32 (1957). It was a grand old building with a swooping tile roof, standing as a traditional sento with more than 70-years of service. Inside, it had undergone only minor changes with newer tiling, but still had in tact the elevated bandai station and an adjacent outdoor garden. Late in the afternoon as it was, more than 30 women of all ages were enjoying their neighborhood bathhouse. Sento in this community was most definitely alive and well.

After waiting for an available place to wash, I started my routine which had developed into a real art form. Everybody has a personal way of preparation, and I was comfortable with mine, as it had become a real form of meditation. Even in the midst of many people, I'd learned how to disconnect from the world by isolating my thoughts and turn everything off around me. In this most private way, the pre-wash step became as enjoyable as the soaking in hot water itself.

Shimizu-yu was special because its hot water originated from a natural hot spring located deep in the ground that came out odorless, tasteless and a dark reddish-brown. The harvest gold tiles with a black-marble trim had given this old sento a modern touch. The water temperature was slightly hotter than the usual 43-degrees. Tokyo is known for its very hot water, and this sento was in keeping with that reputation. After a brief soak, I propped myself up on the marble ledge along with other women doing the same, and dangled my legs in the brown swirl below. Looking across the room, I saw what I thought was a new cooling technique where women were filling their round pails with cold water and sitting with their feet inside the bowls. I'd never been able to fully submerge myself into the cold-water tubs (let alone get past my knees) with temperatures hovering around 15 Celsius, that's just too shockingly cold. So perhaps this cold-water "bowl method" would suit me far better. Since I was always searching for the very best way(s) to enjoy sento, I returned to my wash station and filled my bowl with cold water, but the attempt almost sent me to the wet tile floor in stitches. There was no way my feet would lay flat, even with my toes curled! Alas! Again, my feet were too big! Maybe this was the hint I needed to seriously consider acquiring my own, *extra large* rinse bowl and graduate to the professional leagues of going to sento with my signature bowl. My second cooling option was the private outdoor garden area located out the side door of the dressing area. It was apparent that from the flow of women going in and out, the evening air was refreshing. This outdoor feature is common at sento built in the 20's and 30's. When the grounds are maintained, it's funny how the plants always look exceptionally "lush and green" in contrast to the enormous amount of cold gray concrete found throughout the city.

Just after opening the door, a gray "blur of fur" rushed past my feet. Ah...a clever little feline just waiting for a newbie like me to slide the door wide open and provide her the opportunity to make a run inside the sento. Having no prior knowledge of this kitty's cunning patience, she quickly scurried across the room, over some benches and under a vanity counter. Feeling all eyes upon me, I too jumped across the benches and ended her game, which had everyone laughing as I took the unwanted guest outside. Together we cooled off on an elevated wooden walkway, and I gave her my best behind the ear kitty-scratches, realizing she had already graduated to the professional leagues with a game of "catch me if you can." I'll bet this scene played out daily.

Shimizu-yu exemplified a bathhouse that was in near perfect balance with modern day Japan. In a room filled to capacity, the sights, the sounds and the situations were a slice of sento at its best. Not only did it give me hope that the public bathhouse would survive a little longer, but it was apparent that the people in this neighborhood were not ready to give up their tradition. Within the invisible, yet distinct boundaries of the neighborhoods throughout the city, I was pleased to see the strong support of the public bath in Musashi-Koyama.

Chapter 16

A Force of Change

Last week, I was told the two sento I'd visited only 2-years prior in Chigasaki had closed. Each had been built in the early Showa era, and both had grand architecture serving the beach community near Kamakura. Neither sento had ever installed lockers in the dressing area, opting rather to use large woven rattan baskets on open shelving, a method used since the Edo era. They were classic, beautiful and pure. One of the sento (Ebisu-yu), like Konparu-yu in Ginza, had the most beautiful *kutani* tiling in the entry and also inside the tub area. I don't know the fate of these buildings, nor do I know if saving the tile was even considered. The news had left me feeling quite sad. It seemed ironic that the following weekend I was planning to go to Matsuya department store to see the *ko-kutani* (old kutani) ceramic show, a traveling display of bowls, plates and accessory items from the historic ceramic region. For the most part, this public showing featured pieces from the mid-1600's to early 1700's. The tiles at the Chigasaki sento, on the other hand, were from a more modern era, a time when mass production had been a type of business that had enabled the kilns to survive tough times. I believe it is only a matter of time before these simple story-telling tiles will also be recognized as treasures, not only because of their connections to the oldest kilns in Japan, but because they were a significant part of the vanishing public bath culture.

The new Japan is being defined by a generation born after 1990, and it could easily be said that the changes in society are occurring faster than ever. This group is actively pursuing their own identity and making choices, selecting if you will *what to keep and what to throw out*. Sento is being thrown out. It's considered old-fashioned and for some, even to be avoided. This unpopular status and lack of community support not only left the last two sento in Chigasaki victims of a massive change, but hundreds of others as well. Not everything in life has a Disney story ending.

My search for sento had taken me south to the Island of Kyushu, and as far north as the snow country of Hokkaido. I saw first hand how the old business is struggling with a 21st century transformation. This modern social change differs from that of Meiji Restoration, as well as the dramatic transition that occurred after World War II. Today's sea change is not coming from outside pressures or the government, but *from within*. Of course a young generation has the right to make lifestyle choices, and in their rightful place, it seems certain that going to sento was not going to be included. Just a breath away, for the first time in nearly 400-years, sento will virtually disappear from the neighborhoods of Japan, leaving, for those who adore the business (and I'm not alone) an irreplaceable void. It will soon become a memory, handed down in stories told, old lyrics sung and visits to the Outdoor Edo-Tokyo Museum. In the big picture, forever lost will be the architecture, the bandai, and the common place where neighbors come together to socialize and bathe.

Just as the United States has lost many of its family traditions, such as cutting the annual Christmas tree, sewing the family quilt, or handing down your mother's recipe box, societal change occurs in every culture and on every level. Even though sento has endured for hundreds of years, simply put it's reached the end; and in retrospect, this is probably the number one reason why I'd been so drawn to the last days of its existence.

A few years have passed since my first sento visit, and during this time, I've taken many willing and a few not-so willing visiting foreigners and Japanese to the public bath. Wherever I go, my "sento antenna" is up. I even count the sento stacks while riding the Narita Express train when traveling to and from the airport. My record count stands at 22, and sitting on the left-hand side going northeast seems to be the best seat for spotting the towering landmarks. Usually my departing flight is around 6pm; so heading to Narita between 3pm and 4pm is the perfect time to spot the billowing stacks. Sadly, however, the *active* stack count this last November was only 1.

In 2007 I moved to the Musashi-Koyama neighborhood in Tokyo, a mix of free standing homes, apartments and condos, all of which were built with a bath. Since arriving, one sento has gone out of business, one remains barely open and Shimizu-yu was torn down but replaced with a new updated version. Chances are fairly good this newly remodeled sento will do well because the location is blessed with having natural hot spring water, classifying it as an "onsen," a rare occurrence within the city limits. The neighborhood may have lost its architecture, but hopefully not its soaking tradition.

The cost of a barrel of oil is on a roller coaster of unpredictability. From unthinkable triple-digit prices to below $40 a barrel, there's no mercy - only more punishment for sento owners trying to hang on. These dreaded price swings make planning and projections nearly impossible. I don't want to know the current number of closures this year, and I find myself even afraid to go back and visit some of my favorite locations, as I don't want the disappointment of finding them gone.

In our global society, we can indeed connect faster and easier than ever before using Internet sites like facebook.com, myspace.com, twitter.com, linkedin.com, and for Japan, mixi.co.jp. We are a new breed of community that anyone with an Internet or cell phone connection can join. The explosive growth of these virtual communities has made it convenient to meet and share with strangers, but as easy as it is to join, it's even easier to leave. The on line world is far less complex compared to friendships that involve a face-to-face communication. Personal interaction requires a unique set of social skills, so one feels more at risk. When given the choice of communication methods, it's not surprising that the softer environment of email and text messaging are preferred and rapidly becoming the standard. Don't misunderstand me, I enjoy the convenience of these technologies; they allow me the option to participate when I feel like it, and be a bystander when I don't. It's not sticky. Sometimes this is good! But my point is that the on line community will never replace the sento community.

In these twilight years, for as long as it's possible, I will continue to conduct my mini-sento tours for Japanese friends and visitors from far away. In addition, when given the chance, I will keep asking the older generation, "Do you go to sento?" Because regardless of their social or economic status, they always smile as a memory comes rushing in. Their answers serve as testimony that the humble public bath has played a major role in many personal lives. Moreover, the stories are fun, and they come first hand from a segment of Japanese society who will be some of the last to say, "Yes, I've *been* to sento."

Reference Notes

Books

1. Kokoro, **Hints and Echoes of Japanese Inner Life**
    Author: Lafcadio Hearn
    Publisher: IBC Publishing

2. The New Life with Sento; Sento Style
    Author: Sento Style Promotion Committee, edited by
    Shinobu Machida
    Publisher: Artist House Publishers

3. Sento – The Japanese Public Bath of the 20th Century.
    Photos by Onuma Shoji, supervised by Shinobu Machida
    Publisher: Danvo

4. The Tattoo History: A Source Book
    Author: Steve Gilbert, with Cheralea Gilbert,
    contributions by Tricia Allen, Don Ed Hardy, and Kazuo
    Oguri
    Publisher: Power House Books

5. Yoshiwara: The Glittering World of the Japanese
    Courtesan
    Author: Cecilia Segawa Seigle
    Publisher: University of Hawaii Press

6. The Big Book of Sumo
    Author: Mina Hall
    Publisher: Stonebridge Press

7. Bushido: Legacies of the Japanese Tattoo
    Author: Takahiro Kitamura and Katie M. Kitamura
    Publisher: Schiffer Publishing

8. The Ion Effect: How Air Electricity Rules Your Life and Health
   Author: Fred Soyka, co-author Alan Edmonds
   Publisher: Bantam Books NY

9. Vanishing Japan: Traditions, Crafts, & Culture
   Author: Elizabeth Kirtani
   Publisher: Charles Tuttle Company

10. The Japanese Tattoo
    Author: Sandi Fellman, D. M. Thomas (Designer)
    Publisher: Abbeville Press

11. Dalai Lama: Discourse on the Heart Sutra
    Author: Kozo Otani
    Publisher: Geneon Entertainment

12. The Nightless City (The History of the Yoshiwara)
    Author: J.E. de Becker
    Publisher: ICG Muse

13. Furo - The Japanese Bath
    Author: Peter Grilli
    Publisher: Kodansha Inc.

14. Japan – A Reinterpretation
    Author: Patrick Smith
    Publisher: Vintage Books, a division of Random House

15. Skin Shows: The Tattoo Bible
    Author: Chris Wroblewski
    Publisher: Collins & Brown Ltd.

16. Water Magic
    Author: Mary Muryn

Publisher: Simon and Schuster

17. Travel in the Land of the Gods - The Japan Diaries 1898-1907
Author: Richard Gordon Smith
Publisher: Prentice Hall Press

18. Kotto
Author: Lafcadio Hearn
Publisher: MacMillan Company

19. Cathedrals of the Flesh – My Search for the Perfect Bath
Author: Alexia Brue
Publisher: Bloomsbury

20. Gleanings in the Buddha Fields
Author: Lafcadio Hearn
Publisher: Harper and Brothers 1897

21. Vanishing Japan
Author: Elizabeth & Itsuo Kiritani
Publisher: Tuttle 1995

22. Japanese Only
Author: Arudou Debito
Publisher: Akashi Shoten

23. 70 Japanese Gestures: No Language Communication
Author: Hamiru-Aqui and Aileen Chang
Publisher: Stonebridge Press

24. Discover Japan, Vol.1
A compilation of authors
Publisher: Kodansha International

Sento

Chigasaki:
  Ebisu-yu
  Asahi-yu

Ebisu:
  Shimbashi-yu
  Komyosen
  Hiroo-yu

Fukuoka, Kyushu:
  Miyako-yu

Ginza:
  Komparu-yu
  Tsukishima-yu
  Ginza-yu

Gotanda:
  Manpak-yu

Ikebukuro:
  Sakai-yu
  Shinsaki-yu

Itabashi:
  Yuyu-yu

Kamakura:
  Takino-yu

Kita-Senju:
  Chiyono-yu
  Haruno-yu
  Daikoku-yu

Umeno-yu
Midori-yu
Benten-yu
Takano-yu

Meguro-ku:
Komesen

Minato-ku:
Manzai-yu
Koyama-yu
Tamagiku-yu
Mitsukoshi-yu
Takanawayokujo-yu
Takeno-yu
Fureaino-yu
Koshino-yu

Sapporo, Hokkaido:
Fuji-no-yu
Ki-raku-yu
Showa 30

Setagaya-ku:
Komano-yu
Sakae-yu
Chiyono-yu
Kouzen-yu
Chitose Karasuyama-yu
Masu Ho-yu
Dainichitose-yu
Shiroyama-yu
Yoshino-yu

Shinagawa-ku:
  Hoshino-yu
  Shinsei-yu
  Hachiman-yu
  Komparu-yu
  Nakanobukineu-yu
  Shimizu-yu

Sumida-ku:
  Taisho-yu
  Sumida-yu

Tamagawa:
  Tsubamae-yu
  Komatsu-yu
  Matsuno-yu
  Shinju-yu

Ueno:
  Tsubame-yu
  Taito-yu

Super Sento:
  Oedo Monogatari Onsen, O Daiba

Day Spa:
  Pacific Hotel, O Daiba, Tokyo
  Kyoto Royal Hotel & Spa, Kyoto

Ryokan / Onsen:
  Kansuiro Onsen, Hakone
  Ruka Onsen, Shizouka
  Juban Onsen, Tokyo

Minshukus (Japanese Inn):
  Akebono so, Lake Kawaguchi

Printed Publications

1. 1010 Monthly Sento Magazine, published by the Sento Association of Tokyo

2. Daruma magazine, Summer 2003, Issue 39
   19th Century Kutani Porcelin

3. Japan Quarterly, Jan-March 1999
   The Indelible Art of the Tattoo, Mansfield Stephen

4. The Kofukuji Temple Complex (pamphlet for visitors to Tokondo)

5. Kofuku-ji Kokuhokan (pamphlet for visitors to the Treasure Hall)

6. Kateigaho International Edition, Winter Issue 2006, Vol 10
   Article: The Delights of Ko-Kutani, pursuing a porcelain legend

7. ARTiT Art Quarterly, Fall Winter 2005, Vol 3 No 4, page 47

8. Kateigaho International Edition 2007 Autumn Issue, Vol 17, page 59

Other Sources

1. Edo-Tokyo Museum

2. Edo-Tokyo Open Air Architectural Museum
   Kodakara-yu

3. NHK TV Transcripts "Hokkaido Close Up" – Otaru
   Onsen Lawsuit
   Saturday February 5, 2000.

4. Tokyo Sento Association
   www.1010.or.jp

5. Tokyo Bureau of Welfare and Public Health
   www.fukushihoken.metro.tokyo.jp/

6. Tokyo Life Cultural Bureau
   http://www.shouhiseikatu.metro.tokyo.jp

7. Various archives at the International House of Japan, Tokyo

8. Paintings: Tadanori Yokoo – Artist – Sento Series of paintings 2004

9. Video: Dalai Lama: Discourse on the Heart Sutra by Kozo Otani, 2004
   Published by Geneon Entertainment

10. Tokyo Bathhouse Union

11. Sammy Corporation
    Press Release: September 2004

12. Matsuya Exhibition on the revival of Ko-Kutani, Yoshidaya ware
    Dec. 30, 2005 – Jan. 16, 2006

13. Yumi Atai
    Sento Employee; Shinagawa

14. Jaanus – Japanese Architecture Data Base

Published Articles on the Internet

1. Background on and Benefits of Onsen Bathing Mendy Nitsch
   Kanagawa International Association June 2002
   http://www.k-i-a.or.jp/ts-report/m-report/m-report.htm

2. The Burakumin: The Complicity of Japanese Buddhism in Oppression and an Opportunity for Liberation by Leslie D. Alldritt
   Northland College;Ashland, Wisconsin
   http://jbe.gold.ac.uk/7/alldritt001.html

3. Oriental Irezumi and Occidental Tattooing in Contemporary Japan by Helena Burton, Oxford University
   http://www.bmezine.com/ritual/A10402/irezumi.html
   reprinted on www.nootrope.net with kind permission

4. Japanese Tattooing from the Past to the Present by Mieko Yamada
   http://www.nootrope.net/tebori.html

5. Clinical Implications of Thermal Therapy in Lifestyle-Related Diseases / Graduates of the School of Medicine, Kagashima University in Japan, Sadatoshi Biro, Akinori Masuda, Takashi Kihara and Chuwa Tei
   http://www.ebmonline.org/cgi/content/full/228/10/1245

6. The Japan Forum
   http://www.tjf.or.jp/

7. Japanese Daily Life and Culture
   http://www.tjf.or.jp/eng/ge/ge04ofuro.htm

Internet Sites

1. The National Museum of Japanese History
    www.rekihaku.ac.jp/english/index.html

2. Japan's Living Tattoo Tradition; home page of the tattoo
    artist Shodai Horikoi
    www.page.sannet.ne.jp/ramutyan

3. Body Modification Ezine
    www.bmezine.com

4. The Vanishing Tattoo
    www.vanishingtattoo.com/yokohama.htm

5. Hiriyoshi III – Tattoo Artist Japan
    www.ne.jp/asahi/tattoo/horiyoshi3/index.html

6. Tattoos.com – archived ezines
    www.tattoos.com/articles.html

7. The Japan Tattoo Institute Website
    www.keibunsha.com/

8. The International Sauna Society
    www.sauna.fi/pages/intlsoci.htm

9. Tsubaki Grand Shrine of America & Tsubaki Kannagara
    Jinja
    Shrine Director: Rev. K. Barrish
    www.tsubakishrine.com/test/home.asp

10. Abilt (maker of pachinko slot)
    www.abilit.co.jp/

11. Ofuro - Sento Drinks
www1.kcn.ne.jp/~yoshi223/ofurod/senf00.html
(I recommend a visit to this site)

12. Junichi Bathhouse Diary
www.kimuralab.org/yasunori/sento/mitsukoshi-yu.html

13. The very best "otaku" site, with hundreds of pictures of sento architecture. www5e.biglobe.ne.jp/~wadyfarm/sentou. html

A special thanks to Dorci Leara and Rob Goss for their valuable input and edit.

Please be advised, some Internet sites may have changed or are no longer accessible.

www.ingramcontent.com/pod-product-compliance
Lightning Source LLC
LaVergne TN
LVHW092317080426
835509LV00034B/645